UNPROFANED PURPOSE

A Deep Exploration into the Ministry of the Spirit of Purpose & Prophetic Guide with Prayers to Usher you into a Retreat of Destiny Repair, Realignment and Entry into Purpose

Ebenezer Gabriels With Abigail Ebenezer-Gabriels

Copyright © December 2021 Ebenezer Gabriels
ISBN: 978-1-950579-00-6

Unless otherwise noted, all Scriptures quotations are from the NKJV, NLT, NIV versions of the Holy Bible. All rights reserved. No part of this book may be reproduced or transmitted in any form or by any means, electronic or mechanical, including photocopying, recording, or by an information storage and retrieval system - without prior written permission of the publisher, except as provided by the United States Copyright law

www.EbenezerGabriels.Org
hello@ebenezergabriels.org

Dedication

THE LORD GOD OF OUR PURPOSE
Your Purpose O Lord stands forever
Let your purpose remain in us
Let us remain in your purpose
Right here on earth
And in eternity

Contents

1. Soul and Purpose: The Creation of the Soul — 6
2. Glance into Purpose: The Mystery of Stars — 18
3. Entry into Purpose: Purpose, the Mantle and Influencers — 28
4. The Spirit of Purpose — 36
5. Profanity in Purpose — 53
6. Introduction to Natural Gifts — 65
7. Rules of Gifts — 76
8. Perfecting Gifts for Purpose — 85
9. Purpose in Time — 92
10. Diligence as a Tool for Purpose — 106

11	Faith as a Tool for Purpose	110
12	People as a Tool for Purpose	115
13	Excellence as a Tool for Purpose	126
14	Journaling as a Tool for Purpose	133
15	Promotion as a Tool for Purpose	140
16	The Retreat of Destiny and Discovery of Purpose	149

The Unprofaned Purpose Book

Ensnared, profaned, condemned, bewitched and defeated by the powers of wickedness - These are the affliction of many. When the enemy strips off the radiance, brightness, glory, and riches; there is still left a shadow, from where the voice of Purpose whispers life. The Spirit of Purpose is the untouchable spirit of God in every human commissioned to lead every life to God's purpose.

The book *Unprofaned Purpose* is God's revelatory tool to get readers educated about the Spirit of Purpose and navigate through its pathways; also, a prophetic guide to delivering souls, minds, and senses from the darkness of satan into the mighty revelation of Jesus Christ for the display of His purpose on earth; and serves as a prayer manual filled with hundreds of prophetic prayers to guide you through the retreat of purpose.

In the updated edition of *Unprofaned Purpose*, Prophet Ebenezer Gabriels and his wife, Pastor Abigail Ebenezer-Gabriels uncovers the hidden wisdom of God on purpose and God's agenda to re-ordain daughters and sons back into His grand purpose through the knowledge of Jesus Christ dispersed in the book.

Chapter 1

Soul and Purpose: The Creation of the Soul

Purpose is often confused with milestones and false achievements. The purpose is far from this. A milestone is usually an important marker toward a purpose, while a false achievement is a milestone that's not relevant to a purpose. The subject of purpose is complex, and the simple mind cannot fathom it. Purpose is a spirit of God that is highly guarded and is only revealed by the Holy Spirit and the Word of God. This book was not written to disclose your purpose to you, but to guide you through revelations from the Word of God, the Holy Spirit and ministerial experiences about the paths of purpose, and how to seek God to guide you into your purpose. You will get to understand what purpose is, how the enemy brings profanity into purposes, the ordinances of God concerning purpose and be guided in the Word of God to enter your original God-given purpose.

To get started, we look back into the start of our existence, the day our soul was created. One of the most difficult tasks any human will ever undertake is the search for their purpose.

The Making of the Soul

Before there was the flesh or before we were placed in the womb, we had one-on-one time with the Lord. God went into His secret place to create our souls. This revelation was shown to David in the book of Psalms 139.

Psalm 139:14-16 NKJV
For it was you who created my inward parts; you knit me together in my mother's womb. I will praise you because I have been remarkably and wondrously made. Your works are wondrous, and I know this very well. My bones were not hidden from you when I was made in secret, when I was formed in the depths of the earth. Your eyes saw me when I was formless; all my days were written in your book and planned before a single one of them began. I will praise You, for I am fearfully and wonderfully made; Marvelous are Your works, And that my soul knows very well. My frame was not hidden from You, When I was made in secret,
And skillfully wrought in the lowest parts of the earth.
Your eyes saw my substance, being yet unformed. And in Your book they all were written, The days fashioned for me, When as yet there were none of them.

On this day, the Lord created the soul. The soul is the formless essence of man. The soul can be compared to an invisible and formless memory chip placed into us at the time of creation, which stores God's purpose to be achieved through us on earth. The soul contains volumes of information packets that we need here on earth to fulfill the purposes God placed in us.

Mysteries of Purpose, the Soul, The Scroll, and Covenants

Psalm 139 describes what happened on the day the soul was created. *Your eyes saw me when I was formless; all my days were written in your book and planned before a single one of them began.* The Scripture reveals that God has a copy of our purpose written down in His book. The Scripture further reveals this mystery in Psalm 40:7-8, "*Sacrifice and offering You did not desire; My ears You have opened. Burnt offering and sin offering*

You did not require. Then I said, "Behold, I come; In the scroll of the book it is written of me. I delight to do Your will, O my God, And Your law is within my heart." The will of God is the written purpose of God about us, which is only fulfilled through obedience. The Scripture above notes, "In the scroll of the book it is written of me". This refers to the purpose that was written in the soul about the individual. Every time we walk in the will of God, we are being obedient and following the plans that have been written in our scrolls. This scroll is where the covenant of God with every man is written. This is the book of covenants containing every promise, plan, and purpose of God in any individual. The duplicate copy of this covenant is kept in the soul. Therefore, the discovery of purpose is a burdensome task, and only a few enter into purpose.

The Preservation and Protection of Purpose

God's purpose and agenda on earth are fulfilled through people. These purposes are highly protected and preserved until the souls assigned to fulfill the purpose are ready. Even though children begin to express their purpose early, they still need physical and mental growth and development to manifest their purpose. Purpose is highly confidential, kept secret, and sealed into the souls of humans so that God's plan does not get into the hands of the devil who is always sniffing around to gather heavenly intelligence concerning the plans of God as revealed in Ephesians 3:10 NKJV - *to the intent that now the [manifold wisdom of God might be made known by the church to the principalities and powers in the heavenly places. As a result of this,* God's purposes through humans are sealed in the soul - a highly secured place. This is one of the reasons we were made in secret; God's purpose was concealed in us.

The Revelation of Purpose

One of the hardest revelations to come by is the revelation of purpose. The purpose is so vital that in search of purpose, people would spend time extensively in pursuit of education, academia would ride up and travel wide to the heights and edge of knowledge, and others would buy expensive tickets to get into conferences just to learn about purpose. Despite these hefty investments, purpose has not opened up to some. There's one reason for that; God has chosen to conceal His purpose, and remains just, allowing everyone, regardless of family status, backgrounds to search out their purposes themselves. This explains why parents cannot open up purposes to their children, no matter how much love they have for them, the key to purpose is given to each soul by the Living God, the God of Heaven, the Father of our Lord Jesus Christ.

Hence, when God proposes in His heart to do a thing, He chooses a vessel for the mission and assigns the purpose to the vessel. The assignment is hidden in the soul of the vessel and locked. With the right walk with God, and at the ordained time, the soul releases the purpose that has been stored into it for the vessel to fulfill God's purpose.

The Covenant of Purpose

In this section, we discuss in detail the covenant of purpose. By God's design, purpose is covenantal. It's an agreement God makes with every soul He creates. In secret is every soul made, and in secret did God sign the covenant with every soul He made. There were no witnesses, no parental consent, and no presence of pastors, prophets, elders, and counselors when the soul was made - it was just the soul and God present. So powerful is this covenant that the copy of the certificate obtained on this day was the election of God upon the soul - such that the only way to access this covenant is only through the fellowship of the soul with the Spirit of God's purpose. The original copy of the certificate of the covenant of purpose is in Heaven, written in His books. The covenant of purpose is the second most powerful covenant the soul carries after the covenant of election into God's kingdom. Purpose is highly secured and it is impossible for a man to successfully enter the purpose of another man. God's technology of securing purpose is never seen before, highly encrypted, and DNA-coded and the lock is kept in heaven while the access is obtainable only by the saved soul.

The covenant of purpose is the most powerful covenant placed upon man, and it goes with man throughout a lifetime. These mysteries are revealed in the words of Jesus when He taught His disciples how to pray in Matthew 6:10 - *May your Kingdom come soon. May your will be done on earth, as it is in heaven.* Jesus spoke in parables to His disciples saying, to fulfill your purpose on this earth, you must pray for the will of the Father which has been written and ordained in His book concerning you in heaven to be fulfilled here on earth. As Jesus taught, we must reach out to God to access His book of covenants, where the covenant is preserved to release unto us a way to excel in our purpose.

It was the same revelation about the Covenant of Purpose that John revealed to his disciples in John 3:27 when a dispute broke out amongst John's disciples because Jesus was baptizing people and the crowd was leaving John for Jesus. "John answered and said, "*A man can receive nothing unless it has been given to him from heaven*". The revelation here is that people are only able to access on earth the terms of their contract with God.
This is why the wrongful pursuits of the purposes usually sponsored by the spirit of envy is an indicator that there is revelation lacking on the subjects of covenants, soul, and purpose. When people, especially believers, come to this revelation, they usually enter depths of repentance and begin to seek the mercy of the Lord to show them ways to gain entry into their purpose. A very powerful prayer that invokes God's

response to a call into purpose is: **O God of the covenant day of my creation, let Your will be done on earth over my life, as it is in heaven - in Jesus' Name.** When you say this prayer genuinely, your soul is calling for the fulfillment of purpose and all the help you need to excel in your mission here on earth.

Purpose and Salvation: Why Believers Should Seek Purpose

The quest for purpose is not present in everyone, as a result, not everyone will get to find out or fulfill their purpose. People have the option to walk several paths in life, but only one way leads to purpose. As kids become youth, they begin to think of what they would do in life. By the time they become adults, some go into their chosen careers, businesses, academics, and other interests. The quest for purpose begins when people find that there is no desire for their soul to continue what they do for work in life. This is when many begin to find out that they have studied the wrong courses in school, they undertook the wrong businesses. When this happens, purpose is likely missing. Every believer has a special purpose as seen in the following Scripture - *who has saved us and called us with a holy calling, not according to our works, but according to His own purpose and grace which was given to us in Christ Jesus before time began* - 1 Timothy 1:9.

Two Levels of Purpose

The purpose of every believer is to carry out a special mission for God on earth. We introduce the two levels of purpose in this section.

General Purpose: The general purpose of every believer is found below:

But you are a chosen generation, a royal priesthood, a holy nation, His own special people, that you may proclaim the praises of Him who called you out of darkness into His marvelous light;

1 Peter 2:9 NKJV

This was ordained from the foundation. This is why Apostle Paul said in Galatians 1:15, "*But when it pleased God, who separated me from my mother's womb and called me through His grace*". It is the responsibility of the believer to find out their specific purpose under this general calling.

Specific Purpose: Apostle Paul, after discovering his specific purpose, said in Romans 11:13, "*For I speak to you Gentiles; since I am an apostle to the Gentiles, I magnify my ministry*". His specific calling was to minister to the Gentiles. His ministry was a focused one, and so was his audience. A purpose is specific and detailed with the right focus revealed with clarity. People fulfill a specific purpose under a general purpose.

Tips: Purpose Levels
- There's always a general purpose
- There is also a specific purpose
- Inside the general purpose is a specific purpose

The level of purpose is expanded in upcoming chapters.

Purpose and Eternal Life

We usually get the question, of why unbelievers doing well and thriving in their purpose. Well, not all unbelievers are fulfilling their purpose, but many are. Everyone, whether saved or not, has a soul and a purpose has been assigned to that soul. Many unsaved are fulfilling their purposes today, because they have a soul, and have been able to fellowship their soul through the

Spirit of God's purpose, and then revelation is released, and they run with it. We always respond to that question by the revelation God has given us; if an unbeliever follows Scriptural principles on purpose, they will find it, even though they are unsaved. If a believer is not in alliance with the Word of God and continues to drink from the cup of grace when they should have embraced instructions from the Word of God, they will struggle and hardly enter their purpose.

It is God's desire for believers who are called by His name to fulfill His purpose. The reality today is that many who are known by the name of Jesus are not getting close to their purpose. The promise of eternal life is to those who are saved. It is God's desire for us to be saved and fulfill our purpose. For those who are not saved but fulfill their purpose, it is also a place of eternal ruin and condemnation. We must understand that there is an active purpose of God ingrained in our souls. The challenge for believers who are not fulfilling their purpose is that It is hard to get into heaven without an earthly purpose. The Scripture spoke concerning Moses and how he almost lost His place in the Kingdom of Heaven.

> Yet Michael the archangel, in contending with the devil, when he disputed about the body of Moses, dared not bring against him a reviling accusation, but said, "The Lord rebuke you!"
> **Jude 9:9 NKJV**

Moses received the laws, taught the laws, raised leaders, and led Israel out of captivity, however, didn't enter into the promised land; he almost lost his place in Heaven, until the Lord sent angel Michael to go contend for His soul. If a man like Moses almost lost heaven because he missed the purpose of the promised land, then we need to brace up. There is a report we will call the "Purpose Report", an account we will give to God concerning the results of the assignment He ingrained into our souls. A passing grade will be determined by the fulfillment of purpose, and a failing grade will be determined by the inability to deliver God's purpose on earth. The verdict on the soul of Moses was hanging on His final purpose of entry into the promised land, but for the mercy of God that delivered his soul from eternal destruction.

As we've learned in this chapter, and Psalm 139, there was a day when the formation of our soul occurred, that day, election into eternal life was concluded and purpose was implanted into the soul.

Prayers
for Revelation into Purpose

1. Lord, I thank you for the revelation on purpose in the name of Jesus.
2. I cast out all the spirit of deception from within me in the name of Jesus
3. I cast out the spirit of false purpose in the name of Jesus
4. Father, I cast every satanically manufactured purpose in the name of Jesus
5. I am delivered from every form of false purpose in the name of Jesus
6. I am delivered from the false purpose the enemy manufactured for me, in the name of Jesus.
7. Lord Jesus, I pray you open to me the revelation of my purpose in the name of Jesus.
8. Lord, let all spirit of confusion be taken out of my life in the name of Jesus
9. The Spirit of purpose is welcome into my life in the name of Jesus
10. Father, let your purpose rise in me in the name of Jesus
11. Father, restore my soul to your intended plan for your use, in the name of Jesus.
12. Father, possess my soul into your original purpose, in the name of Jesus.
13. Lord God, let my soul be connected to your presence afresh, in the name of Jesus.

14. My Father, give me the understanding of my purpose on earth in the name of Jesus.
15. My Father, open to me, the revelation of my purpose to me in the name of Jesus.
16. Lord Jesus, reconnect my soul back to purpose if there is a disconnection in the name of Jesus.
17. Lord let my soul be delivered from the snare of the fowler, in the name of Jesus
18. Father, deliver my soul from the hands of traders of soul in the name of Jesus.
19. Lord Jesus, let my soul escape from every net in the name of Jesus
20. My soul, receive the touch of God in the name of Jesus

Journal

Chapter 2

Glance into Purpose: The Mystery of Stars

Every child coming into the world carries a light with them. This light is the revelation of Jesus which is given to everyone coming to the world for direction into purpose. The last words of John 1:9 share this knowledge.

> *There was a man sent from God, whose name was John. This man came for a witness, to bear witness of the Light, that all through him might believe. He was not that Light, but was sent to bear witness of that Light. That was the true Light which gives light to every man coming into the world.*
> **John 1: 6-9 NKJV**

That ray of light shines from the soul where purpose resides. The form of purpose is reflected in this light, the features of purpose are revealed through light. Sometimes based on the brightness of the light, the weight of God's glory to be revealed through the purpose can be determined. There are a lot of spiritual inquiries made either by parents, grandparents, families, friends, or neighbors about the purpose of a new child, and sometimes through ungodly and illegal routes. Seers may see a distant shining star, representing what the child is to become in the future, but the exact purpose of a child is usually hidden in the child's soul. When inquiries are made into purpose, sometimes, the inquirer may only see the light which is the reflection of purpose around a child, and this can be used to determine the level of greatness of the purpose. However, in all of these, the light doesn't reveal the exact purpose or the pathway to get to the purpose. This happened to Jesus as seen in the Scriptures below.

> *Now after Jesus was born in Bethlehem of Judea in the days of Herod the king, behold, wise men from the East came to Jerusalem, saying, "Where is He who has been born King of the Jews? For we have seen His star in the East and have come to worship Him.*
> **Matthew 2:2-3 NKJV**

Jesus: His Purpose and His Star

The Lights: Light in this context is found in the above Scripture, *"He was not that Light, but was sent to bear witness of that Light. That was the true Light which gives light to every man coming into the world"* - Everyone coming to the world has a light of Jesus within them. This light is revealed when they shine in their purpose. This is why the Scripture instructs in Matthew 5:16 *Let your light so shine before men, that they may see your good works and glorify your Father in heaven.* Jesus told the *disciples in Matthew 5:14, "you are the light of the world",* hunting them about their purpose on earth.

The Star: The star are symbolic representations of the glory of God an individual carries which is manifested through their purpose. This was seen in the example of the star of Jesus mentioned above. Jesus also had the same light with Him when He came as man. This light in Him is called the star. The wise men, by the wisdom of God, knew the written purpose that was aligned with the star of Jesus, and when He arrived on earth, they received signals and went to worship Him. The purpose of Jesus was disclosed long before He was born, and that brought a risk into His purpose. The purpose of Jesus had been declared through the mouths of the prophets as seen below:

> *But you, Bethlehem Ephrathah,*
> *Though you are little among the thousands of Judah,*
> *Yet out of you shall come forth to Me*
> *The One to be Ruler in Israel,*
> *Whose goings forth are from of old,*
> *From everlasting."*
> **Micah 5:2 NKJV**

Looking carefully at the Scripture above, the general overview of the purpose of Jesus was prophesied, but it was not disclosed in plain words. Similarly, purpose can be perceived but the specific purpose is only revealed to the soul carrying the purpose.

A Star: Representation of A Child

God spoke to Abraham concerning stars. He compares the descendants of Abraham to the number of stars shown to him in the sky. The question to ask here is, does it mean each star represents one child? Likely so.

> *Then He brought him outside and said, "Look now toward heaven, and count the stars if you can number them." And He said to him, "So shall your descendants be."*
> **Genesis 15:5 NKJV**

The book of John 1:9 confirms this, as it says, *That was the true Light which gives light to every man coming into the world.* This verse pointed to Jesus as the One who gives light to every man being born. The Scripture further confirms that the star is a type of light in Genesis 1:16-17, *Then God made two great lights: the greater light to rule the day, and the lesser light to rule the night. He made the stars also. God set them in the firmament of the heavens to give light on the earth.* The purpose of the star is also to give light to the earth. Receiving light on earth would mean receiving information from heaven to bring solutions to the earth.

As stated earlier, every child is given a star as they come into the world. This star is given by the Lord Jesus as stated above in John 1:9. The star is the light of purpose. The star contains a lot of information concerning a child, although it doesn't reveal a child's main purpose to others. For this reason, Satan gravitates toward children whose stars have more radiance than others. When the parents are believers, the Holy Spirit sensitizes and informs the parents of the rule of life that would guide the child into God's purpose. One of the earliest rules of life given to Joseph concerning Jesus was to take Jesus into hiding because Herod was set to destroy the purpose Jesus came to fulfill as written in Matthew 2:13.

The Spirit of Herod

The Scripture records, "When Herod the king heard this, he was troubled, and all Jerusalem with him". Matthew 2:2-3. As discussed in Chapter 1, the major reason why God conceals the purpose of people is to guard against envy which may bring destruction, if unchecked, to the vessel carrying the purpose in their soul. The light of the purpose (the star) Jesus carried at the time of His birth was so powerful that his star served as a navigator to the physical location of Jesus. We review this in the Scripture below:

Matthew 2:9-10 NKJV
When they heard the king, they departed; and behold, the star which they had seen in the East went before them, till it came and stood over where the young Child was. When they saw the star, they rejoiced with exceedingly great joy.

The spirit of Herod is the spirit that seeks to ruin purposes. The spirit of Herod is usually at work whenever any individual is about to enter or in the infancy of their purpose. The spirit of Herod seeks to destroy an individual carrying a purpose, the purpose, and those around the individual. To protect Jesus from the destructive powers of Herod, his parents were instructed to hide him in Egypt.

"Now when they had departed, behold, an angel of the Lord appeared to Joseph in a dream, saying, "Arise, take the young Child and His mother, flee to Egypt, and stay there until I bring you word; for Herod will seek the young Child to destroy Him."
Matthew 2:13 NKJV

Astrology and Perversion of Lights

Astrology studies the heavenly bodies such as stars to gather information on humans, purposes, times, and seasons, as well as the agenda of God. Astrology did not begin in the satanic realm. It began with God showing Abraham what He is set to do using the stars as a reference. For thousands of years, prophets of God knew that God showed signs through the stars and other heavenly bodies, as Jesus said to the Pharisees in Luke 12:54-56 - *Then He also said to the multitudes, "Whenever you see a cloud rising out of the west, immediately you say, 'A shower is coming'; and so it is. And when you see the south wind blow, you say, 'There will be hot weather'; and there is. Hypocrites! You can discern the face of the sky and of the earth, but how is it you do not discern this time?* Jesus taught that knowledge can be gained through the study of the celestial bodies. It was through the signals given by the stars and deep studies that the wise men were aware of the birth of Jesus and led them to the place where he was born. However, perversion entered into this realm when the devil took the knowledge and began to use it against people. The infiltration of darkness into the heavenly bodies was addressed in the following scripture:

> *"Keep on, then, with your magic spells*
> *and with your many sorceries,*
> *which you have labored at since childhood.*
> *Perhaps you will succeed,*
> *perhaps you will cause terror.*
> *All the counsel you have received has only worn you out!*
> *Let your astrologers come forward,*
> *those stargazers who make predictions month by month,*
> *let them save you from what is coming upon you.*
> **Isaiah 47:12-13 NIV**

From the Scriptures above, there are agents of darkness using satanic powers to predict and alter the destinies.

Children and Purpose

In many cultures across the world, when a child is born, parents and relatives seek information on the future of the newborn. Mature Christians ask the Lord for revelation through the Holy Spirit while the unbelievers seek revelation through satanic mediums. To get information about the purpose of a child, they may deploy witchcraft practices, hire stargazers or psychics to read palms, and do all sorts of ungodly acts to gain knowledge about the future of the child. Unholy access to a child's star can bring profanity into the purpose of a child. This is the reason why it is highly dangerous for satanic agents to have access to the star of a child because once they do, they begin to craft schemes to profane the purpose of the child.

Satanists seek to know these two major pieces of information: What is the purpose of this child and What is the rule that governs this purpose? Once they have their hands on this confirmation, they look for ways to impact the nurture of the child against the guidelines set by God. The powers of darkness understand that anytime the guiding principles of a child's life are not followed, the purpose of that child will be locked up by the Lord because God is highly protective of His purpose. As a result, many adults have been misled into abominations against their purpose. This is why children whose souls are in a state of purity are more likely to catch a glimpse of their purpose than adults whose souls may have been compromised. Children usually have the privilege of the revelation of the state of their soul, the discovery of purpose is also very related to connection with the soul. The only holdback is that children have to go into the stages of growth and development to enter into purpose. This is why children utter words like, "*I want to become a .... when I grow up. Or This is what I'll do..*" These are not mere random statements, but revelations from the soul. As close as children are close to the revelation of their purpose, they are also in the utmost delicate place. Hence, it takes anointed parents and caregivers to help nurture children on the path of their purpose.

By the time children grow into adulthood, most times they have strayed off the path of purpose because they didn't have the help, they needed to live by God's guidelines for them. Some lessons taught unknowingly to childhood have drawn people farther from their purpose. Many adults today who had a meeting with purpose in childhood somehow slipped away and got into the wrong careers, marriage, relationships, business, and out of touch with God's plan for them. However, in God's mercy, the way to purpose can be re-traced, and the lost road to purpose in childhood can be found, and this is why God has released the book UNPROFANED PURPOSE.

Prayers
to Restore the Light of Purpose

1. Father, reestablish my way into purpose, in the name of Jesus.
2. Father, set my soul back into its purpose, in the name of Jesus.
3. Lord Jesus, let the light you gave to my soul in the foundation of my life be rekindled in the name of Jesus
4. Lord Jesus, let my gloomy star receive your light afresh in the name of Jesus
5. My star, receive the power of the Holy Spirit in the name of Jesus
6. Thou my star, hear the word of the Lord, you are no longer available for the manipulation of darkness, in the name of Jesus.
7. Thou my star, hear the word of the Lord, you will no longer yield to the summoning of darkness in the name of Jesus.
8. Thou my star, hear the word of the Lord, begin to work according to God's plan from the foundation of my life in the name of Jesus
9. Thou my star, do not subscribe to the monitoring of darkness in the name of Jesus.
10. Thou my star that has been covered by darkness, break out of darkness and begin to glow by the light of the Lord Jesus.
11. Fire of darkness lit up in demonic gatherings against my purpose, be snuffed out by the fire of the Holy Spirit in the name of Jesus.
12. The fire of my purpose will not be snuffed out in the name of Jesus.

13. Father, rekindle the fire of my purpose in the name of Jesus.
14. Every licensed strong man that has obtained access and the bill of right to divert my purpose, Lord revoke the access and destroy them, and expel them from my life in the name of Jesus.
15. Thou spirit of herod, you shall not lay hands on my purpose in the name of Jesus
16. Lord, let my purpose be hidden away from the powers of herod in the name of Jesus.
17. Life shall not be snuffed out of me in the name of Jesus

Journal

Chapter 3

Entry into Purpose: Purpose, the Mantle, and Influencers

What is Purpose?

We define purpose as an act of bringing to effect God's agenda on earth accompanied by the display of an array of God's glory including His holiness, light, beauty, honor, wealth, power, excellence, and knowledge in His Word. Purpose, as a spirit of God, is embodied and manifested in these attributes of God, and never dies.

The Mantle of Purpose

Each person is assigned a purpose of God to fulfill, when they complete their portion of God's purpose, the baton is handed over to the next chosen candidate. While praying with a brother, the Lord showed a mantle that was about to be transferred, the Lord told him that a very prominent person in his life was about to depart, and he needed the mantle for his next assignment. A few weeks later, his spiritual father was gone. The death of a person is usually not the end of a purpose. The spirit of purpose hands over the mantle to the next person ready for the purpose. In the next chapter, we study the spirit of purpose in debt.

The Burdensome Doorway into Purpose

God has established pillars to stir us into purpose. The parents, the family, the nurture, and the communities all play an important role in influencing the entry of people into their purposes. However, there's one challenge, the earth is in such an aggressive state of bondage, thereby threatening purposes and making it difficult to become fulfilled. The Scriptures speak about the difficulty in fulfilling the purpose which we examine below;

> *I consider that our present sufferings are not worth comparing with the glory that will be revealed in us. For the creation waits in eager expectation for the children of God to be revealed. For the creation was subjected to frustration, not by its own choice, but by the will of the one who subjected it, in hope that the creation itself will be liberated from its bondage to decay and brought into the freedom and glory of the children of God. We know that the whole creation has been groaning as in the pains of childbirth right up to the present time. Not only so, but we ourselves, who have the firstfruits of the Spirit, groan inwardly as we wait eagerly for our adoption to sonship, the redemption of our bodies. For in this hope we were saved. But hope that is seen is no hope at all. Who hopes for what they already have? But if we hope for what we do not yet have, we wait for it patiently.*
>
> **Romans 8:18-25**

The world is a place of decay needing liberation. The liberation of the decayed is possible only when the children of God fulfill their purpose. The Scripture above noted, *"the glory will be revealed in us"* which denotes the fulfillment of purpose. The revealing of the children of God is the display of God's purposes in His children. Addressing the difficulty of entering purpose, we look at the following words from the Scripture, *"the creation was subjected to frustration"*. Many people encounter roadblocks and become frustrated while attempting to find or fulfill their purpose. The Scripture above *"the creation itself will be liberated from its bondage to decay and brought into the freedom and glory of the children of God*", teaches that a successful entry into purpose by God's children ushers liberation into the world. Whenever an individual enters the realm of purpose, the world records an invention, innovation, or some important type of breakthrough.

Influencers of Purpose

God has designed influences of people, self, community to assist on the way into purpose. When God's design is followed, people enter purpose. The devil's goal is to deceive and mislead out of the path of purpose and has set up evil designs to achieve that. The common influencers of purpose are named below.

Family Background: God selects children into their families. Children do not get to choose their families. While no one knows God's selection process, this process reveals the Just attribute of God. Children are carrying powerful purposes of God who have come from families that appear incompetent to help nurture the child towards purpose. Also, there are children from very humble backgrounds who have grown up to become world-changers. This reveals the Justness of God. The Scripture below explains further:

> *"Woe to him who strives with his Maker! Let the potsherd strive with the potsherds of the earth! Shall the clay say to him who forms it, 'What are you making?' Or shall your handiwork say, 'He has no hands'? Woe to him who says to his father, 'What are you begetting?' Or to the woman, 'What have you brought forth?'* .
> **Isaiah 45:9-10 NKJV**

The above Scripture notes that God selects according to His will. Family backgrounds can advance or deter a purpose. Many children who were privileged to glance into their purpose lost it when their parents unknowingly shut down their visions of purpose. Some children are anointed creators ready to bring forth new methodologies and technologies to the earth but were discouraged from purpose by their parents unknowingly.

Self: The self is also one of the influencers of purpose. When an individual enters full maturity. their lifestyle, habits, and decisions made will further establish them or dethrone them out of purpose. The following are the major factors leading self out of purpose
1. Entry into a state of rebellion
2. Submission to wrong mentors
3. Wrong associations
4. Bad decisions
5. Disobedience to the Word of God

Election by Salvation: The election of God upon a person's life from the foundation is influential to entry into purpose. Election into salvation is ordained, and when a believer is elected, they are called to fulfill God's purpose on earth. Believers are elected for a purpose - to fulfill God's mission on earth. Hence, when God's children become saved, joy abounds in heaven. God becomes delighted when His children discover their purpose and work in it. Likewise, God does not rejoice when the elect fails to get into purpose. The great thing about the election by salvation is that regardless of family background, even when a person is born into idolatry, they are removed from darkness into the light of God. Also, God makes provisions for a new life once the elect enters their appointment into salvation. These new provisions become the pillars of purpose.

The Pillars of Purpose

The pillars of purpose support everyone who has been elected to fulfill the purpose of God. Where the pillars of purpose are absent, there's no framework to provide the support needed to guide into purpose.

#1: Word of God: The Word of God are instruction and revelation sets available to guide every purpose that is to be fulfilled under heaven. The Word of God came into existence before the foundation of the world and is the foundation of the life of the believer.
Counsel
Instructions to activate your gifts

#2: Wisdom of God: The Wisdom of God has all the know-how we need to make decisions and sound judgments in the will of God. Wherever the wisdom of God is lacking, the purpose of God is missing in there.
Counsel to translate into what you need to do
How to make critical decisions

#3: Worship: Worship is every activity that we do that delights, God. Every form of communion, including prayers, is worship unto the Lord. A prayer is also a form of worship. One of the expressions of worship is studying. The Scripture says, "*The works of the LORD are great, Studied by all who have pleasure in them*" - Psalm 111:2. When we get into the mindset that every activity that delights God is worship, then many of our actions are fashioned towards the will of God, which is the purpose of God.
The condition of your mind, actions, lifestyle all put together is worship

#4: Time: Every purpose to be fulfilled is written in time. This is written in Ecclesiastes 3:1 - *The works of the LORD are great, Studied by all who have pleasure in them. A purpose is surrounded by time.* People who are not fulfilling their purpose are simply

wasting time outside of the arena of purpose. Anyone who would enter purpose has a mastery of their time and a revelation into how to use their time per season.
Doing the right things at the right time,

#5 Being in the right place at the right time. Some places do not support your purpose. Some places do not support your calling.

Prayers

for Establishing the Pillars of Purpose

1. Lord Jesus, make right every wrong foundation in the name of Jesus
2. Lord Jesus, visit the foundation of my family with your power in the name of Jesus
3. Father, establish the pillars of my life in the name of Jesus
4. Let the pillars of my life that are wobbling be strengthened in the name of Jesus
5. Father, every broken-down pillar of my life is rebuilt in the name of Jesus.
6. Father, deliver my purpose from obscurity in the name of Jesus.
7. Father, deliver me from the captivity of purpose in the name of Jesus.
8. Father, deliver me from the influence of my foundation that has locked me outside the gates of purpose, in the name of Jesus.
9. Father, deliver me from the influence of my foundation upon my advancement into purpose, in the name of Jesus.
10. Father, deliver me from the influence that has blocked my vision to purpose, in the name of Jesus.
11. Father, deliver me from the voices in my foundation that has led me gently but wickedly away from my purpose in the name of Jesus.
12. Lord, deliver me from the relationships that have turned me into the enemies of your purpose for me in the name of Jesus.

13. My Lord, let there be a divine announcement with my purpose in the name of Jesus.
14. My Father, bring me into the courtroom of my purpose where the scroll of my purpose will be revealed unto me in the name of Jesus.
15. Lord, let me not run on other's benchmark in the name of Jesus
16. My Lord, let me only walk in my timeline in the name of Jesus.
17. Father, teach me how to put time to use in the name of Jesus
18. Father, overshadow me with the spirit of Your wisdom in the name of Jesus
19. Father, send me helpers of destiny that will influence my purpose for good in the name of Jesus.
20. My Father, let worship rise from within me in the name of Jesus.

Journal

Chapter 4

The Spirit of Purpose

God's Perspective of Purpose

In this chapter, we're looking at purpose from God's perspective. As satan continues to redefine purpose, the worldview of purpose is distorted, leading many to mistake false achievements for purpose. When this happens, profanity is introduced to a purpose. This is why we are called to carefully search out our purpose and fulfill it.

What is the Spirit of Purpose?

Purpose has its own spirit and is called the Spirit of Purpose. The Spirit of Purpose is one of the four spirits of God that is given to man at the time of creation. Three of the other spirits are often talked about. The purpose is the fourth and the least understood. The purpose is a Spirit of God assigned to man to carry out a specific plan of God on earth. Three major spirits work closely with the spirit of purpose. In the next section, we discuss them.

ANALYSIS OF GOD'S SPIRITS IN MAN

#1 - Conscience: A Spirit of God

There is a Spirit of God residing in the core of man. It is called Conscience. Conscience is always alive and responsible for whispering the iniquity of the sinner to them saying, "what you are doing is bad". Conscience speaks all languages. If you're

German, conscience will speak to you in German, If you're Russian, it will communicate with you. Everyone can hear their conscience speak to them.

The devil deceived Adam and Eve that they would come to the knowledge of good and bad if they ate the fruit from the forbidden tree. In other words, they would develop a conscience. He said to them, "*For God knows that when you eat from it your eyes will be opened, and you will be like God, <u>knowing good and evil.</u>*" Genesis 3:5. They already had good knowledge from the beginning. Looking at what happened right after God created all the animals, Adam knew the right names for each of the animals and named them accordingly. Genesis 2:19-20 *records -* "*Now the Lord God had formed out of the ground all the wild animals and all the birds in the sky. He brought them to the man to see what he would name them; and whatever the man called each living creature, that was its name. So the man gave names to all the livestock, the birds in the sky and all the wild animals*". Adam was already filled with the knowledge of good, and he did not need the knowledge of evil. The following Scripture notes that the introduction of the law ushered in sin.

What shall we say then? Is the law sin? Certainly not! On the contrary, I would not have known sin except through the law. For I would not have known covetousness unless the law had said, "You shall not covet." But sin, taking opportunity by the commandment, produced in me all manner of evil desire. For apart from the law sin was dead. I was alive once without the law, but when the commandment came, sin revived and I died. And the commandment, which was to bring life, I found to bring death. For sin, taking occasion by the commandment, deceived me, and by it killed me. Therefore the law is holy, and the commandment holy and just and good.
Romans 7:7-12 NKJV

In Adam and Eve's case, there was no law, until they fell. Also, conscience was activated in them after they had fallen.

At the time they fell into sin, conscience kicked in. The conscience calls people to an awareness of sins and anything that obstructs the will of God.

#2 - The Preservation of Life

The Spirit of Preservation of Life is a spirit present in every person. When people are faced with life-and-death scenarios, the natural tendency is that they look for ways to survive. No human being in their right mind will choose death. Also, when people are in danger, they usually call people around for help, and the instinct will be that the people around help or call others who can help. The underlying reason why we want our lives preserved is that there is a purpose to be fulfilled. This spirit is highly associated with the spirit of hope, which looks forward to the promises of God.

#3 The Spirit of Creativity

The spirit of creativity is one of God's spirits which is embedded in the spirit of wisdom. God sent Adam and Eve into the fallow ground and gave them the ability to create for survival. Creativity allows us to bring solutions to existing problems. With the spirit of creativity, people create art, designs, buildings, machines, and innovations that have not been seen before. With the spirit of innovation, a never-seen-before strategy is created to move a nation forward. The Scripture teaches about the ways of creativity in Exodus 31:1-5 *"Then the Lord spoke to Moses, saying: "See, I have called by name Bezalel the son of Uri, the son of Hur, of the tribe of Judah. And I have filled him with the Spirit of God, in wisdom, in understanding, in knowledge, and in all manner of workmanship, to design artistic works, to work in gold, in silver, in bronze, in cutting jewels for setting, in carving wood, and to work in all manner of workmanship*". Bezalel was a man who had the spirit of creativity in him, this spirit was needed to help fulfill the purpose of God (building the temple) which Moses had received. The spirit of creativity is one of the spirits that fuels purpose. For every purpose to be fulfilled, the spirit of creativity is needed.

#4 - The Spirit of Purpose

Purpose is a spirit responsible for guiding into the manifestation of God's divine agenda. The Spirit of Purpose has been in man since the soul was created. Unlike the other 3 spirits, the spirit of purpose is the quietest of all and the most powerful. The spirit of conscience is always talking, the spirit of creativity is exciting, while the spirit of the preservation of life is always watchful and aggressively protects God's life in people. The spirit of purpose is not quick to speak because it is a very private spirit. This is why it is hard to find purpose. Solomon spoke concerning a purpose in Ecclesiastes 1:13 - *And I set my heart to seek and search out by wisdom concerning all that is done under heaven; this burdensome task God has given to the sons of man, by which they may be exercised.* The moment a person discovers their purpose, the purpose of purpose begins to scream loud and roar, rejoicing in a divine purpose that has been fulfilled, and bringing into fulfillment the Scriptures found in Romans 8:18-19 *"For I consider that the sufferings of this present time are not worthy to be compared with the glory which shall be revealed in us. For the earnest expectation of the creation eagerly waits for the revealing of the sons of God".* The world is changed and full of joy whenever the purpose of God is fulfilled on earth. False achievement does not compare to purpose, it is a talkative and noisemaker spirit boasting outside of purpose about a purpose it has no awareness of.

Overview of the Design of Purpose

Purpose is often confused with milestones. Some equate a false achievement to purpose. Back in 2018, we ministered to an individual; they kept losing jobs, finances not in order, getting sick, and things were shutting down on them. God said, pray for them like this: *Lord, remember the covenant of the day of conception and turn situations around for good.* They continued with this prayer, and God showed up in mighty ways. This prayer called us into a place of looking back on the day of conception.

The Covenant Day of Conception

As discussed in Chapter 1, there was a day before we were made when God planned out all our days on earth. This was before we were formed or planted in our mother's womb. Psalm 139 describes the covenant of the day of conception. It was the covenant that was made by the Lord with the creation. King David said, " In secret, the Lord made me". On this day, God created each person without consulting their parents, pastors, and prophets - it was just God by Himself. This was the day of assignment of purpose and the covenant day of conception. This day precedes the moment we were placed in our mother's womb. This mystery is revealed below:

> *For it was you who created my inward parts; you knit me together in my mother's womb. I will praise you because I have been remarkably and wondrously made. Your works are wondrous, and I know this very well. My bones were not hidden from you when I was made in secret, when I was formed in the depths of the earth. Your eyes saw me when I was formless; all my days were written in your book and planned before a single one of them began.*
> **Psalm 139:14-16**

On the day of creation, there is a covenant God forms with man. That covenant is written in the Books. That covenant is the most powerful covenant placed upon man, and it goes with man throughout a lifetime. These mysteries are revealed in the words of Jesus when He taught His disciples how to pray in *Matthew 6:10 - May your Kingdom come soon. May your will be done on earth, as it is in heaven.* Jesus spoke in parables to His disciples saying, to fulfill your purpose on this earth, you must bring to God's remembrance in prayers that He has written about you on your covenant day of conception. Our purpose was ordained in heaven, and not on earth. As Jesus taught, we must call on heaven, where the covenant is preserved to release unto us a way to excel in our purpose.

A very powerful prayer that invokes God's response to a call into purpose is: O God of the covenant day of my conception, let Your will be done on earth over my life, as it is in heaven - in Jesus' Name. When you say this prayer, you are calling home to send you help to excel in the mission given to you. When life comes to a standstill and a believer prays to God and says, O God of my purpose, reset my life to your original plan for me, in the name of Jesus. The results, things reset, and a new blessing is released. This prayer supersedes the prayer your mother or father can pray for you. As a believer, if you know that there was a day that there was before your mother conceived you, you can beckon to the covenant made on that day with God, and God honors.

It is the same secret of the covenant day of conception John revealed to his disciples in John 3:27 when a dispute broke out and they said Jesus was baptizing people and the crowd was going to Jesus. "John answered and said, "*A man can receive nothing unless it has been given to him from heaven*". The revelation here is that people are only able to access on earth the terms of their contract with God on the day of conception. If many believers have access to the revelation of the covenant day of conception; the culture of hate will be extinguished, and more people will seek the Lord to show them ways to gain entry into their purpose. Yahweh knows the hearts of men He created have made it impossible for a man to successfully enter into the purpose of another because the purpose is DNA coded, and the key of purpose is kept in heaven.

The Way of Purpose

Think of the spirit of purpose as a living being standing behind a door in a house. The owner of the purpose is outside the house looking for ways to enter the house, but the spirit of purpose will not open the door to its owner until the person meets certain requirements.

Now you're on earth. You need to find the path that leads to your purpose. Unfortunately, the ways to purpose are usually not clear, and not every way that appears to lead there is the right way. The Scripture notes - *There is a way that seems right to a man, but its end is the way to death.* - Proverbs 16:25. This is so because God made it that way because He is just and fair. We must then set out to search for the wisdom to look for the right way to get to our purpose. Purpose is hidden as a glory to God and purpose is searched out as out by those honored with the glory of God as Proverbs 25:2 reveals - *It is the glory of God to conceal a thing: but the honor of kings is to search out a matter.* In the search for the fulfillment of our purpose, we must understand that by default, the world makes things look as though there is no purpose, or a purpose is unachievable. We must not be deceived.

Everything that God made is waiting with excitement for the time when he will show the world who his children are. The whole world wants very much for that to happen. Everything God made was allowed to become like something that cannot fulfill its purpose. That was not its choice, but God made it happen with this hope in view: That the creation would be made free from ruin—that everything God made would have the same freedom and glory that belong to God's children.

Romans 8:19-21

From the above Scriptures, we see that the nature of purpose is complex. God created our purpose before He created us. God then places us in a corrupt wicked world, one filled with the decay of corruption and shackles to fulfill a purpose. Yet the creations of God are expecting the revelation of God's purposes in us. The fulfillment of purpose is the clear wall that separates God's children from those who are not His. Purpose reveals to the world who the children of God are. The day of the unveiling of purpose is the day of the announcement of sonship to the world. The main goal of purpose is to reveal the purpose of God on earth. manifestations of God's glory on earth.

What Does Purpose Look Like?

We can only identify purpose if we learn the ways of purpose. In this section, we at the attributes of purpose

#1 Purpose is Obedient: God's agenda is usually communicated to individuals. Obedience to the Holy Spirit will lead you to your purpose *"For those who are led by the Spirit of God are the children of God"* -Romans 8:14. Without obedience, there is no purpose. Only those who obey will diligently carry out each assignment of God and will be called the children of God.

#2 *Purpose Is Holy*

Purpose is the glory of God and it is adorned with holiness. If you ever desire to walk into purpose; go in the way of holiness. Purpose resides in the soul. When profanity gets into the soul, the soul becomes unholy, and where there is unholiness, the spirit of God departs from there. Where there is no spirit of God, there is no revelation into purpose. If there is any revelation whatsoever, it is a revelation from the pit of hell. The revelation puts people into further bondages. The spirit of God sets free. Where there is holiness, purpose opens.

#3 Purpose Is Time-Sensitive

There's a time for every purpose. All our childhood days are preparation for purpose. Purpose These are the years of the spirit of purpose Many people hear the voice of purpose in their spirit man, but they cannot tell it is purpose speaking to them. The purpose usually sounds alarm bells when people are growing up and they feel that time is running out without any achievements. The purpose is highly time-sensitive. Purpose is ever working in time and when people suddenly feel there is a need to use their time wisely, it is the voice of purpose speaking to them concerning time. When people waste time, the voice of purpose is screaming from afar. Ecclesiastes 3:1 reminds us: *To everything there is a season and a time to every purpose under heaven.*

This is the song that Purpose sings to people, it only has 4 verses;

> *I am waiting,*
> *I am screaming,*
> *when do you want to wake up,*
> *time is running out*

#4 Purpose is Emotional, Empathetic & Helpful

The Spirit of Purpose is emotional. As a Spirit of God, the Spirit of Purpose has its emotions. In Ephesians 4:30, we are told not to grieve the Holy Spirit of God. The spirit of purpose cries out when people's ears are blocked from the truth.

Purpose is responsible for nudging us to take actions that are in alignment with God's will for our lives. Spirit as the Spirit of Purpose takes charge. Sometimes, purpose cries out from within, when people are walking contrary to God's plan. The spirit of purpose becomes grief. Sometimes purpose leads people into the right relationships and communities that will set them free from bondage.

When the spirit purpose observes that an individual is disobedient or living in bondage outside of purpose, it begins to lead them to places where they need to hear the Word of God or places where they will meet with an anointed vessel of God, especially true prophets that will catch a revelation into God's plan and speak by the authority of God to open the revelation of purpose to them. The spirit of the individual's purpose will be the spirit of the prophet when the Lord opens the eyes and ears of His prophets. The prophet's assignment is only to unlock the overview of the purpose and release the authority for the individual to enter the doors of purpose. From that moment onward, some people's eyes will be opened, and they will begin to take progressive steps toward their purpose from that day.

As for individuals who are still under the foundational curses in Romans 8:20 *against its will, all creation was subjected to God's curse.* These curses follow them around to wherever their purpose pushes them to seek help. Purpose pushes people out whispering to them, *"you need to attend that prayer conference, you need to go to worship now, you need to go to the deliverance program,"*, knowing that the Spirit of Purpose will be there to speak through the mouth of the ministers to them. Purpose pushes people to where they will find help to walk into their purpose. Sometimes they get to a prophet who has been granted access to the Lord's presence and an overview of their purpose. When the Lord reveals their purpose through the mouth of prophets, some of them will look at the manual God gives to them and throw it out of the window, disdaining the voice of their purpose. Such people hear that purpose and immediately despise their purpose.

The second way the foundational curse works against people's purpose is by luring people into the net of false ministers, satanic prophets, and demonic gatherings where they are fed with lies and lured into more complicated problems. Though people's lives are melting away and getting rotten, they will hardly wake up to this reality. Some people in this category receive God's mercy and hear God's voice in dreams in the form of a warning so they can wake up and be realigned to purpose before it is too late.

#5 Purpose Is Transient

The spirit of purpose inhabits the living. The spirit of purpose only works with the living. One of the ways you can check to see whether a purpose was fulfilled or not is to look for the continuity of work after the one who originally did the work departed the work. Purpose does not abide with man the moment after breath departs. Purpose does not go to the grave with the dead. The moment a person of purpose departs from the world; the spirit of purpose looks around for another person who is walking deeply in God; when purpose locates that person, purpose jumps at that person. That is one of the concealed meanings behind the word of God in *Proverbs 10:7 - The memory of the righteous is a blessing.*

In a recent encounter, I was shown the vision of a servant of the Lord who is advanced in age. In that vision, I saw the man doing the work of a painter and in his hands was a green liquid. Then I saw that he began to wash his hands as if he had finished his painting job. Then the Lord said to me, his time is coming to an end. The Lord said concerning him, he is a man without blemishes, one whom the Lord has helped in walking the walk of salvation safely and circumspectly. The Lord said he has fulfilled his purpose but there is no one who is ready to receive the mantle for continuity.

Back in 2016, the Lord spoke to one of our friends. The Lord told me to ask them what the name Joseph *(not real name)* means to them. They said Joseph was an influential person in their lives. The Lord said Joseph is done with his assignment and getting ready to pass the baton to them; and in a few weeks, they called to say Joseph had passed away. The work of purpose lasts beyond a generation. There is continuity and a multi-generational plan for God's true purposes. When a person living in purpose is about to go be with the Lord, the spirit of purpose looks for the next person; if no one is fit, purpose never compromises, It waits until another person is found to carry on the mission.

#6 Purpose Provides Guidance

Through its voice, the Spirit of Purpose guides people. When people are wasting away, Purpose will whisper phrases like, *"before you can get to where I am, go into the presence of God"*. Some people will say they heard in their mind a voice speaking to them on how to get a solution or giving them direction. That is the voice of purpose. The moment a person successfully meets with purpose, purpose overshadows them. Any individual working for God's purpose is very passionate, and nothing can stop the purpose in them as they become dangerously focused. They become a soldier enlisted into the arena of Purpose, who would not be stopped until every mission is accomplished. Nothing can stop them from the purpose of God. The spirit of purpose is like a sibling of the spirit of purpose. When the door of purpose is closed, the spirit of purpose screams, "Read this book, there's something I want to open up to you through this book", so that you can attain the wisdom to enter into the door of purpose. Sometimes purpose leads people into worship and whispers, "worship the Lord now for the spirit of wisdom to be released".

#7 *Purpose is Irreplicable*

Purpose is unique to the one whose soul has been assigned to the purpose. God is a Creator and has numerous purposes. Hence the Purpose of God for a soul cannot be duplicated. The unique purpose of God for every individual cannot be transferred to another person until they die. When people come to this understanding, the attempt to take over the purposes of others sparked by envy will die. When people scheme to take over the purpose of others, purpose is locked up and the ultimate attainable success a schemer will attain is false purpose. This is why no one who steals the work of others, or ideas of others will ever fulfill God's purpose through it, hence the warning in Exodus 20:17 CEV *Do not desire to possess anything that belongs to another person--not a house, a wife, a husband, a slave, an ox, a donkey, or anything else.* - the Spirit of Purpose does not support covetousness.

#8 Purpose Is Aggressive
Purpose is aggressive. When purpose finally opens to a person regardless of age; purpose becomes very aggressive and rapidly comes into display because of the time that has been wasted. If a 70-year-old discovers purpose at 70 and is supposed to fulfill a purpose from when they were 30 years old, the spirit of purpose can get very aggressive. The moment purpose meets them at age 70 and assuming they have about 20 more years to live, purpose will rush them and fulfill through them all the work of 40 years in as fast as 10 years. This is how aggressive the spirit of purpose can be. When God said to Joshua in Joshua 13:1, "*You are old, advanced in years, and there remains very much land yet to be possessed.* It was God's attribute and voice of Purpose that was speaking to Joshua, reminding him that though much has been conquered, there are many more to conquer.

#9 Purpose Is Not A People-Pleaser
At a point in the life of King Saul people said, "*Is Saul also among the prophets*" because he was prophesying. When Saul's tenure expired, the Lord closed all the channels previously used to speak to Saul. The day that the Lord stopped speaking to Saul by Urim or Thumim or by the prophets was the day that the fire of

his purpose was quenched. When Prophet Samuel spoke to Saul; It was the Spirit of Purpose speaking to Saul, dialoguing with his spirit man "I already knew from the day you came to meet me that you love God that men, that you love men more than your soul. Saying you love man more than your soul. If a person seeks to please people for the fulfillment of purpose, they would rarely last inside of purpose. People-pleasing and purpose do not go well, purpose throws out people who are only interested in pleasing others over what is right.

Prayers
for Alignment into the Ways of Purpose

1. Lord, place my feet into the paths of purpose in the name of Jesus
2. Father, align me with your purpose amplifiers In the name of Jesus.
3. Lord, let your spirit of purpose guide my ways in the name of Jesus
4. This is the season of the breaking forth of purpose, therefore, let my head, let my heart and the entirety of my being work in alignment with purpose.
5. This is the season of purpose reality, in the name of Jesus
6. This is the season of purpose application, in the name of Jesus
7. Let my soul, mind, spirit and body begin to work hand in hand with purpose, in the name of Jesus.
8. Shield my life from the wind of sorrow, in the name of Jesus
9. Shield my purpose from the wind of sorrow in the name of Jesus
10. Lord my Father, locate me with your gentle mercy in the name of Jesus.
11. Lord, heal my soul and lead me back into purpose, in the name of Jesus.
12. Foundational powers blocking my ears and ears to purpose, be destroyed by the power of resurrection in the name of Jesus.

13. Lord opens my ears to the voice of purpose in the name of Jesus.
14. Let the voice of purpose communicate clearly to me in the name of Jesus
15. Lord my Father, clarify my purpose to me in the name of Jesus.
16. Father, let my lost purpose be found and given to me in Jesus' name.
17. O God my Father, locate my life with the wonders of purpose, in the name of Jesus
18. Restore unto me the glory of my purpose, in the name of Jesus.
19. Let there be a restoration of purpose, in the name of Jesus.
20. Father, open up my mind that your spirit of creativity may flow into me in the name of Jesus.

Unprofaned Purpose

Journal

Chapter 5

Profanity in Purpose

Purposes does not die, but profanity can be introduced into a person's purpose. In this chapter, we look at what profanity in purpose looks like, and discuss the ways the enemy is profaning the purposes of many. The purpose is profaned when God's will can no longer be fulfilled by an individual because they have been intercepted and polluted. When profanity enters a person, mission, place, or business, the spirit of profanity replaces God's purpose concerning that person, mission, place, or business.

How Purpose Becomes Profaned

In previous chapters, we learned that the components of purpose live in the soul. If ungodliness enters a soul, purpose becomes locked up, and the soul is no longer able to assess its original purpose and tends towards a false purpose.
happened to the sons of Aaron in the Scripture below:

> *Then Nadab and Abihu, the sons of Aaron, each took his censer and put fire in it, put incense on it, and offered <u>profane fire</u> before the LORD, which He had not commanded them.*
> **Leviticus 10:1 NKJV**

The KJV version of Leviticus 10:1 says:
And Nadab and Abihu, the sons of Aaron, took either of them his censer, and put fire therein, and put incense

thereon, and offered <u>strange fire</u> before the Lord, which he commanded them not.

One version describes the kind of fire as profane, the other calls it strange. We look at the context in which these two words were used to derive their meanings. In the times of Aaron, Priests prepared incense in alignment with the recipe revealed by the Lord. A strange fire occurs when the instructions are not followed, perhaps there was a wrong mix of incense, a strange component used in the worship of other gods was added to the incense for the worship of Yahweh, or perhaps, it was a type of offering not commanded, or they were not supposed to worship in the manner they did. This concept of strange fire applies to purpose. Only God has the blueprint for your soul, the moment the soul is introduced to elements that are not in alignment with the blueprint, profanity begins.

What is Profanity?

Profanity is unholiness or uncleanness as described by the Scripture in Ezekiel 44:23, *And they shall teach my people the difference between the holy and profane and cause them to discern between the unclean and the clean.* The Lord is holy. So is His Spirit. The purpose of God is holy and will not abide in unholiness. Where there is no holiness, there is uncleanness, and the purpose of God cannot dwell in an unholy soul. This is why the righteousness of Jesus Christ is needed for the purification of the soul.

Indicators of Profanity in Purpose

Profanity has entered the soul if...

#1 Closed Vision: Where there is closed vision, there is no visibility into purpose. One of the indicators that profanity has set in is when individuals are confused and have no revelation for the future. This could mean there is no revelation released from the Lord, or it could be that God is speaking but the individual is not hearing the voice of God.

#2 Blurry Vision or Confusion: Some people may have glanced into purpose and suddenly confusion sets in and unable to go further in. Confusion enters the mind for many reasons, most especially when there is a compromise with your walk with God which has allowed the devil to take over the mind.

#3 Unholy Sexual Engagement: When people are involved in sexual engagements outside of marriage and have not sought the Lord in true repentance and deliverance - *Leviticus 21:9 - The daughter of any priest, if she profanes herself by playing the harlot, she profanes her father. She shall be burned with fire.* Any form of sex outside of marriage will have profane purposes. While some go ahead to get married, profanity still exists in the foundation of that marriage, until deliverance is obtained.

#4 Lack of Advancement: Whenever profanity sets into an individual, business, or ministry, there's no progress. This is why the devil usually sends polluting powers to pollute people, missions, and businesses to hinder advancement. into a place, there is no moving forward, whether in an organization, in a team, in a place, business, or ministry.

#5 Wrong Marriage: Profanity sets in if you have wrongfully married the wrong spouse, who was not part of God's plan for you. The wrong spouse will bring along profanity, without not much that can be done. The mission of many satanic agents is to lure people into the wrong marriage because this is one of the easiest ways to pervert purpose. When this error is committed, profanity enters. Satanic spouses like that will do everything possible to ensure that their victims do not grow tangibly with the Lord and frustrate the purposes of God in their spouses.

#6 The Wrong Use of the Tongue: Profanity sets in when people have no control over their tongues. The Scripture teaches 2 Timothy 2:16 -*But shun profane and vain babblings: for they will increase unto more ungodliness.* All forms of gossip, participation in wrong conversations, false testimonies, lies, and speaking to destroy the reputation of others are reasons why profanity enters into purpose. There is a spirit that backs up every word spoken. It could be the Spirit of God or the spirit of darkness. Speaking falsehood and pulling others down with words are major blockers of purpose.

#7 Satanic Involvement: All forms of participation in satanic groups, affiliation with mediums, witchcraft, sorcerers, consultation defile purpose. Ezekiel 23:39 - *For when they had slain their children to their idols, then they came the same day into my sanctuary to profane it; and lo, thus have they done in the midst of my house.* When individuals consult satanists or accept membership in witchcraft groups. Purpose departs. There's an individual God brought to us. The individual carries a powerful purpose of God. However, when they came for prayers, God said to tell them: *Why have you sought after other gods? Was my name not enough to deliver you or is there no God in Israel that could deliver you? As long as you continue in that witchcraft group, there is no entering into purpose. There's no way you can enter into your assignment and my plan for you with your continuity in that group".* Like this individual, many people went into the occultic thinking life would become better for them, only to get in there and find themselves in bigger trouble. One of the most painful parts of this is that some who have occultic involvement are people who had been called and elected as ministers of God. Many of them had joined the occultic before they came to know there was an election of God upon their lives. Some proceed even further into ministry despite their active occultic involvements, and they cause further damage to people's destinies. Whenever there is an involvement with the satanic, there is no entry into purpose, because God will never share His glory with any other.

#8 Extreme Hardship: One of the indicators of a profane purpose is extreme hardship. Lack of revelation sometimes leads people to wrong and unauthorized choices, and that brings blockage in all that they do. When life is unusually hard and there seems to be no room for breakthroughs, it may be that profanity has entered. It is never God's plan for His children to be in extreme hardship. Jeremiah 29:11 says *"For I know the plans I have for you,"* declares the LORD, *"plans to prosper you and not to harm you, plans to give you hope and a future.* God has not ordained darkness to triumph over His children. When there is no conception of good things, no birth of goodness, no inflow of favor, no pattern of progress, the purpose might have been profaned.

Soul Transaction: A Transaction to Profane Purpose
One of the main reasons why the soul is the main point of attack for the enemy is because the soul is the place where purpose dwells. To profane an individual carrying God's purpose, the devil looks for the weakest link to enter the soul. God gave Ezekiel a strange word to deliver, and the word introduces us to the subject of soul trading and profanity.

> *"Likewise, son of man, set your face against the daughters of your people, who prophesy out of their own [heart; prophesy against them, and say, 'Thus says the Lord God: "Woe to the women who sew magic charms on their sleeves and make veils for the heads of people of every height to hunt souls! Will you hunt the souls of My people, and keep yourselves alive? And will you profane Me among*

My people for handfuls of barley and for pieces of bread, killing people who should not die, and keeping people alive who should not live, by your lying to My people who listen to lies?" 'Therefore thus says the Lord God: "Behold, I am against your magic charms by which you hunt souls there like birds. I will tear them from your arms, and let the souls go, the souls you hunt like birds. I will also tear off your veils and deliver My people out of your hand, and they shall no longer be as prey in your hand. Then you shall know that I am the Lord. "Because with lies you have made the heart of the righteous sad, whom I have not made sad; and you have strengthened the hands of the wicked, so that he does not turn from his wicked way to save his life. Therefore you shall no longer envision futility nor practice divination; for I will deliver My people out of your hand, and you shall know that I am the Lord."
Ezekiel 13:17-22

The only way purpose can be profaned is if access is given to darkness into the soul. God called to question the workers of iniquity, questioning their dirty works of soul hunting. Then God asks, "*Will you profane me among my people*"? This means, will my purpose in the captive souls be profaned? Access to purpose is highly dependent on the state of the soul. One of the fastest ways people open up their souls to soul hunters is when they become susceptible to lies stated in the underlined Ezekiel 13 verses quoted below:

> Will you hunt the souls of My people, and keep yourselves alive? And will you profane Me among My people for handfuls of barley and for pieces of bread, killing people who should not die, and keeping people alive who should not live by <u>your lying to My people who listen to lies</u>?" '

Anytime the soul is opened up to lies, manipulation, immorality, unholiness, satanic ideas, and ungodly philosophies -

if the soul is not filled with the power in the Word of God to wade off such corruption, profanity enters into it.

Soul Transaction: Wrong Philosophies

Philosophies contending against the Word of God brings pollution to the soul. Some ancient philosophers were idol worshippers, and some of their philosophies were totally against the Word of God. These philosophies impact the belief systems of people and cause them to live a life based on these foreign beliefs. We find in the Scripture below the activities of Epicurean and Stoic philosophers in the times of Apostle Paul;

> *Now while Paul waited for them at Athens, his spirit was provoked within him when he saw that the city was given over to idols. Therefore he reasoned in the synagogue with the Jews and with the Gentile worshipers, and in the marketplace daily with those who happened to be there. Then certain Epicurean and Stoic philosophers encountered him. And some said, "What does this babbler want to say?" Others said, "He seems to be a proclaimer of foreign gods," because he preached to them Jesus and the resurrection.*
> **Acts 17:16-18**

In the book of Acts as quoted above, there was an idol-infested city and it turned out that there were also philosophers in the city. When the Apostle Paul shared the gospel of Jesus with them, they thought it was one of those philosophical ideas. The Epicurean philosophy belongs to the school of thought that the soul is made of atoms and space, this is based on the idea of disbelief in the existence of God. The Stoic philosophy is the ideas that get people to get into ungodly meditations, ungodly ways of sourcing for peace, and similar ideas. A lot of different philosophies have been adapted into self-help therapies and some have made it into some church pulpits. Many quotes that have been adopted as people's life philosophies or guiding principles have become the ruling force of people's destinies. Some of these quotes exalt the self above God, giving a false sense of achievement or pride.

There are some ancient philosophers who believed there was no purpose to life. Many of their writings were carved out of their major idea that there is no purpose to life, hence, when a believer chooses to subscribe to a quote coming out of the idea that there is no purpose to life, what happens is that the words they believe become their reality. Jesus said in John 6:63 - *The words that I speak to you are spirit, and they are life.* When people follow ungodly philosophies, their mind is fashioned after that philosophy, and the spirits backing those philosophies dominate the mind, as a result, the purpose of God does not stand in those situations. Our beliefs are very important to God, just as it was written in John 3:36 - *He who believes in the Son has everlasting life, and he who does not believe the Son shall not see life, but the wrath of God abides on him.* Consequently, ideas are very powerful, and we must watch out for the ideas we allow to transform our minds.

Prayers
for Deliverance from Profanity

1. Father, revisit my soul with your mercy, in the name of Jesus.
2. Father, look upon my soul with your favor once again in the name of Jesus.
3. Father, reveal to me every source of profanity in the name of Jesus.
4. Lord, open up every closed vision in the name of Jesus.
5. Lord Jesus, sanctify me with your blood from every pollution resulting from unholy sexual engagements in the name of Jesus.
6. Father, deliver my soul from the wrong use of my tongue in the name of Jesus
7. Deliver me from extreme hardship in the name of Jesus
8. Father, show me the agents of corruption assigned against my soul in the name of Jesus
Father, let my soul receive life, by the power in the body and flesh of the Lord Jesus.
9. Father, let your breath come into my spirit afresh in the name of Jesus.
Father cleanse my soul with your blood in the name of Jesus
10. Lord Jesus, wash my soul with your Word in the name of Jesus
11. Father Lord, let my soul receive deliverance from the marketplace of darkness in the name of Jesus
12. Father, deliver my soul from satanic ideologies in the name of Jesus.

Father, deliver my soul from soul trading in the name of Jesus.

13. My soul, receive the firepower in the Holy Spirit and break free from the coven of darkness in the name of Jesus
14. My soul, be set free from the bondage of lies in the name of Jesus.
15. My soul, receive the breath of heavens in the name of Jesus.
16. My soul, receive the power from on high in the name of Jesus.
17. My soul, you are dedicated to the Lord as holy in the name of Jesus.
18. Every strange fire in my soul, be quenched by the fire of the Holy Spirit in the name of Jesus
19. The Lord shall increase my capacity for retention of good things, in the name of Jesus
20. No longer will I be a one-star wonder. I will continue with diligence to retain great things in the name of Jesus.
21. The scepter of honor has been released. The kingdom has been given to you
22. I shall not miss my ordination in the name of Jesus.
23. The scepter of the kingdom has been released unto you.
24. The Lord has released strength, He is the pillar of your strength.
25. Lord, release unto me strength to enter into purpose in the name of Jesus.
26. Lord, fill me with the confidence of the Holy Spirit to step forward to do what you have been called to do.
27. I receive strength upon strength for entrance and dwelling into purpose
28. Usher my life into your prominence in the name of Jesus.
29. Lord purify my life in the name in the name of Jesus

30. The root of bitterness is uprooted from my purpose in the name of Jesus.
31. Let a realignment with my destiny occur in my life, in the name of Jesus
32. Every polluted stream in my life, let the blood of Jesus be released into those streams in the name of Jesus.
33. Lord Jesus, break all types of entanglement, manipulating my purpose, in the name of Jesus

Journal

Chapter 6

Introduction to Natural Gifts

What's a Gift?

Natural gifts are tools for performing tasks leading to purpose. They are the abilities given to us to fulfill a mission. Natural gifts are fueled by the Holy Spirit. Every gift is from God, and every time God issues a gift, He never withdraws it. The Scripture notes that the gift of God is without repentance. Natural gifts must be nurtured for them to multiply and produce fruits. God has given us gifts to become fruitful.

> *"For it will be like a man going on a journey, who called his servants and entrusted to them his property. To one he gave five talents, to another two, to another one, to each according to his ability. Then he went away. He who had received the five talents went at once and traded with them, and he made five talents more.*
> **Matthew 25:14-16**

In the parable of the talents, the ones who were able to produce more with the gifts received more, while the ones with lesser fruits received less.

The Role of Gift in the Fulfilment of Purpose

Every gift is given for a purpose. A gift is one of the tools needed to fulfill one's purpose. However, gifts do not always come fully developed. Gifts are usually covered up and must be unwrapped and refined before it can be used for a purpose. This is why many raw gifts never fulfill a purpose. It takes hard work for gifts to be developed and the power of God for gifts to find its matching purpose. Gifts can be released to an individual without the individual using the gift for anything of value. When an individual with a set of gifts is unable to put the gift to fruitful use, they are likely unskilled.

Types of Natural gifts

There are two types of gifts:
1. Active Gifts: Active gifts are gifts that have been found, developed and functioning for purpose.
2. Passive gifts. Passive gifts are discovered or undiscovered gifts, and both have one thing in common: they are not functioning towards a purpose yet. Passive gifts are broken down into two.
    a. Passive undiscovered gifts are gifts that have not yet been discovered yet.
    b. Passive discoveries are gifts that have been discovered that have not been exploited.

Announcement of Gifts

When gifts are active in a person's life, that gift has been discovered, refined, and polished by the individual. Once the carrier of the gift is aware and has proven prudent with the use of the gifts, the voice of God begins to speak to announce the gift. Just like in the case of Moses, when the Lord directed Him to build a temple and gave Him the pattern. The Lord gave Him requirements to follow, and He also announced the men whom He had blessed with the gifts that could fulfill that requirement. One of those men was Bezalel:

The Announcement of the Gift of Bezalel

Then the Lord spoke to Moses, saying: "See, I have called by name Bezalel the son of Uri, the son of Hur, of the tribe of Judah. And I have filled him with the Spirit of God, in wisdom, in understanding, in knowledge, and in all manner of workmanship, to design artistic works, to work in gold, in silver, in bronze, in cutting jewels for setting, in carving wood, and to work in all manner of workmanship.
<u>Exodus 31: 1-5</u>

God never allows His gifts to go unused. He gives gifts, nurtures gifts, and also announces the gift. The pattern given to Moses needed the skills of Spirit-filled artisans. Moses needed more than a skilled builder. He needed builders who were tuned into the mind of God and God helped Moses out in His search. He called Moses' attention to someone already in His network, opening the eyes of Moses to the gifts deposited into the life of Bezalel.

A vital lesson to learn about God's gift is that it is never to manipulate to bring God's gift into prominence. The Scripture says *a man's gift will make room for him* - Proverbs 18:12 not the other way round. When a person begins to make room for their gifts, God is no longer the backer of the gift, the devil has taken over. The Holy Spirit counsels, empowers, enables, defends, and announces gifts. This was what came into play in the life of Bezalel. This is why gifts can only come into the limelight when God allows others to discover them. A person who is blessed with a gift cannot effectively announce their gift as the Scripture notes in Proverbs 25:27, "It is not good to eat much honey; So to seek one's own glory is not glory".

Gifts are needed to complete the next assignment to get promoted into the next phase towards the direction of purpose. Knowing one's giftings is the basis of the discovery of purpose. To search out purpose, search out what gifts have been released to you. What gifts are manifesting within you? The gifts that are released to us are the vehicle that we ride into our purpose

Parents and Gifts

Godly parents are the only persons privileged to have an idea of what the purpose of their children is through the gifts they observe in the lives of their children.

Jesus received worship and scented aromas

When they heard the king, they departed; and behold, the star which they had seen in the East went before them, till it came and stood over where the young Child was. When they saw the star, they rejoiced with exceedingly great joy. And when they had come into the house, they saw the young Child with Mary His mother, and fell down and worshiped Him. And when they had opened their treasures, they presented gifts to Him: gold, frankincense, and myrrh.
Matthew 2:9-11 NKJV

Mary, the mother of Jesus, was privileged to see her son welcome the wise men, and they brought gifts to Him. The first was the gift of worship. God is the One who receives worship, and that could have given Mary a clue about what her son's purpose on earth was.

Incubation of Gifts

Jesus' gifts went through a time of incubation. The incubation time was when His gifts were not ready to be put to work for a purpose and needed to be kept out of public notice. This is addressed in the Scriptures below when the mother of Jesus knew Jesus had the spiritual gifts to fix a problem at a wedding.

Jesus said to her, "Woman, what does your concern have to do with Me? My hour has not yet come."
John 2:24

Jesus noted that the hour to manifest His giftings has not yet come but his mother placed a demand on the gift which He honored. This is another lesson on the concept of timing and gift. There is a time of incubation of gifts given by God. It is a time when the gift is discovered, nurtured, and then birthed to life for a purpose, just like embryos are developed within an egg. If gifts are expelled without proper incubation or at the wrong timing, gifts can be hijacked by satan or misused.

As discussed in earlier sections, God's gift is irrevocable, but satan always tries to hijack gifts. This is why some worshippers started as choir members in the church, but they have been lost to the world and have become prominent tools used by the devil to spread pornography and demonically inspired music. The devil knows the Lord does not withdraw his gifts, so he tries to snatch people away from the ways of God and divert their gifts for his use.

The proper incubation timing must be completed before a gift is announced. Times of incubation may be lonely times for the carrier of the gift. There may also be times when the gifted go through refinement, such that God takes away impurities that may bring pollution to the gift. For others, the time of incubation is a time of testing for readiness. It was not clear how Bezalel's gifts came into full development; however, Bezalel was a former slave in Egypt, and that gave him a lot of time to put his gifts into practice.

We say to people, never abandon the gifts because your gifts have not been announced yet. The timing is an opportunity to grow your gifts, protect your purpose and find out what your gift is needed for her on earth.

Container and Gift

Human beings are like containers. When containers are not used, it can get dormant and rusty. If care is not taken, other things can take over it. The Scripture establishes that God does not take back His gift - *the gift and calling of God are without repentance* - Romans 11:29. A container can only take to the extent to which it is designed to take. If you pour oil into a container and you also add water to the same container, the water struggles to displace the oil, and the oil struggles to get rid of the water. The volume of water that the container can contain hasn't changed but the content is gradually changing to what is being poured in, and the dominant content will stay. We must always walk in the awareness that the gifts in us are in a container (us), and we must do everything to protect ourselves and stay away from pollution.

Multiplication of Gifts

Gifts can be multiplied. Elisha was the leader of the prophets. The younger prophets were drinking from the wells of the School of the Prophets under the leadership of Prophet Elisha. The lead prophet would teach on the prophetic ministry, thereby showing them how they can function in their own gifts. The newly realized gifts of these younger prophets began with the one who started a school and discovered his own original gifting. This is how the multiplication of gifts works when a person develops gifts in other people through the gifts in them. It's called the multiplication of gifts.

Another instance where we see the multiplication of gifts is in the situation of the elders of Israel.

Multiplication of Gifts

So the Lord said to Moses: "Gather to Me seventy men of the elders of Israel, whom you know to be the elders of the people and officers over them; bring them to the tabernacle of meeting, that they may stand there with you. Then I will come down and talk with you there. I will take of the Spirit that is upon you and will put the same upon them; and they shall bear the burden of the people with you, that you may not bear it yourself alone.
Numbers 11:16-17 NKJV:

The burden was taken off Moses, and God told Him to designate elders of Israel who will share in the gift of God's spirit upon the life of Moses. God took some of His Spirit upon Moses and shared amongst the elders so that they would receive gifts to continue Moses' assignment for the purpose of God given to Moses. The gift of God can be extended, just as it was extended over the life of the elders of Israel from Moses. Here is why a divinely gifted person does not run out of gifts, because gifts can be multiplied.

Manifestation of Gifts

We are called to reveal the glory of God in us - to manifest God's purpose by using our gifts. The manifestation of our gifts works towards achieving a purpose. Those who use their gifts effectively will eventually walk in their purpose. A person may discover they have the gifts of observation. They may begin to question the composition of air for example and eventually find that some air types are more dangerous to inhale. They may go ahead to publish their findings and help the government create a policy around that to prevent public exposure to dangerous gases. God's original purpose for this person may be to educate the world about air types and save lives by presenting safer options and methods of air use. His purpose was fulfilled, but it all began with mastering the gifts of observation. To manifest our gift, we must be in full submission to the Lord. The manifestation of gifts and the spirit of humility works together. Where there is humility, a gift in an individual will lead an individual into the next milestone on the way to their purpose.

Pride is one of the reasons why God abandons gifted individuals. When the spirit of pride comes upon gifted individuals, they may begin to exalt their gifts over God. This is where the self-exaltation philosophy comes to destroy people.

When a person worships their gifts, the Lord stops backing that gift and satan takes over the control of that gift. At this point, they begin to manifest all forms of pride which eventually leads to destruction.

Prayers
for the Preservation of Gifts

1. Father, visit my soul with your purity in the name of Jesus
2. Let the power of your mercy deliver my gift from every form of captivity in the name of Jesus.
3. Lord, show me every hidden gift you have placed in me, in the name of Jesus.
4. Lord, let my spirit be manifested for your glory in the name of Jesus
5. Lord Jesus, let your power protect your gift in my life in the name of Jesus
6. Every dormant gift in my life, receives the resurrection power of the Lord Jesus.
7. Every gift of God in my life currently in the hands of darkness, let the finger of God retrieve it unto me in the name of Jesus.
8. Every gift wrongly channeled be realigned by the power of God in the name of Jesus.
9. Lord announce your gifts in my life in the name of Jesus.
10. Father, let the gifts you've given me open doors for me, in the name of Jesus.
11. Let me gifts be activated in the name of Jesus
12. No longer shall my gifts slumber in the name of Jesus
13. Father, connect me to helpers of destiny that will enhance my gifts in the name of Jesus.
14. Father, connect me with helpers of destiny that will help transform my gifts in the name of Jesus
15. I am delivered from the spirit of pride in the name of

Jesus
16. My gift shall not turn me to the enemy of God in the name of Jesus.
17. I will not share God's glory with anyone, in the name of Jesus.
18. My gift shall not suffer corruption in the name of Jesus
19. Father, separate me from powers that seek to swallow my gifts in the name of Jesus

Ebenezer & Abigail Gabriels

Journal

Chapter 7

Rules of Gifts

God gives gifts, and the Spirit of God is responsible for powering gifts. Gifts are very sensitive and there are guiding principles that must be observed around gifts.

Rule 1: Gifts are carefully hidden and are only discovered by others or situations. The carrier of the gift is unable to open the gift up by themselves.

Rule 2: Gifts are salvation neutral. The saved and both unsaved have gifts in them.

Rule 3: Gifts are natural abilities given to us, and always need exploration and deep cultivation before it can fulfill a purpose.

Rule 4: Natural gifts should not be mistaken for spiritual gifts; they are on two different pathways and for different purposes and cannot be substituted for one another to fulfill a purpose.

Gift Openers

Gift openers are the instruments of opening or discovering gifts.

The Word of God: The Word of God is the most potent tool to enhance your gift. While your gift may be buried deep, the Word of God will always locate your gift because the Word is powerful and precise enough to penetrate the realm of the soul and spirit. The Word of God brings understanding into the mind and explains what gift is in a man. The Word of God enlightens people about their purpose and helps them identify the gifts in their lives that translate into purpose. The Word of God helps open gifts because purposes are decreed by the Word of God.

As a result, anytime we fellowship in the Word, this is the birth of new ideas because the Word opens the realm of wisdom, wealth of knowledge, breakthroughs and new possibilities.

The Living Church - active in the power of the Holy Spirit - is a gift opener. This is why many famous musicians started from the church. The Scripture notes in Ephesians 3:10 - *"to the intent that now the manifold wisdom of God might be made known by the church to the principalities and powers in the heavenly places".* Where there is a living Church, a spirit-filled church - there is the abundance of God's gifts being unveiled. God's agenda on earth is disclosed to the church, especially through prophets. When God's agenda is being revealed, participants of such fellowships, churches, gatherings, conferences are spiritually awakened, and minds are opened, and they begin to see how their life can fit into the general purpose of God. As a result, they suddenly wake up to the realization of the gifts they need to fulfill the promises of God. Also, through the gifts of revelation from the Holy Spirit, gifts can be discovered. We remember a brother who came with his family for prayers. God said to tell him "you're a pilot". He says, "No I'm not, I am an HR professional". Some months later, he got admitted into the US Navy, and was being trained as a Naval pilot.

Points of Affliction by the Enemy - Points of affliction, persecution, hate, and opposition are usually fertile ground for the discovery of gifts. The Lord uses the enemy to shake His people out of complacency. This is usually the place of the discovery of gifts. The Jews are so little in number compared to other giant nations with large numbers of people, yet they lead the space of technology because they have worked hard on exploring, testing, and perfecting their gifts. Limitations of scarcity are some of the tools the Lord uses in helping people find their fit. Like Joseph said to his brothers who afflicted him into greatness in the book of Genesis 50:20, *"But as for you, you meant evil against me; but God meant it for good, in order to bring it about as it is this day, to save many people alive".* Many successful people who worked God's wonders with their gifts were pushed into the discovery of gifts at the point of enemy affliction. Singapore has no natural resources, and they have space limitations, yet they are one of the top financial powers in the world.

Research: Asking and Seeking: One of the ways people discover their gifts is by asking and active research. When people go into research, they are looking for new information that can lead to new knowledge. This is provided by God's Spirit of wisdom. The Spirit of wisdom is released for people to search out information that they will need to get into the work for their purpose. Man research leads to further research or development of an idea or product. In the process of development, gifts are found. King Solomon was a researcher. He researched, and his research led to many writings, development, and wisdom. Through some of his research, he found:

> *The locusts have no king, Yet they all advance in ranks -*
> Proverbs 30:27;

> *Righteousness exalteth a nation: but sin is a reproach to any people. Proverbs 12:34*

Gift Lockers

Gifts can also be locked up by the actions and lifestyles of people. God determines to close up gifts when certain rules are broken, and boundaries crossed. We discuss the gift closers in the next section.

Lack of the Word of God: Where there is insufficient Word of God in individuals, gifts can be locked up. The Word of God has the power to connect the soul back to God for revelation, and when that is not happening, people seek worldly wisdom which leads to nowhere.

Wrong Atmosphere: When an individual is in a perpetually sorrowful state, gifts will be locked up. The spirit of creativity works in a joyful atmosphere, as a result, where the atmosphere is heavy and there is no joy, gifts are locked up and difficult to access.

Closed Mind: People whose minds are not open to freshness never get their minds renewed. A closed mind is never interested in new revelations. This is a dangerous place to nurture gifts, as a result, they mostly are unable to discover gifts needed to fulfill purposes.

Forces of Discouragement: Agents of discouragement are used by satan to whisper negativity into the minds of people. They gently discourage, manipulate, and lead away from the activities which foster the discovery of gifts with the goal of perverting purpose. Some people share ideas with people for validation, and they get results like; "you're out of your mind", "you think you're the first person to do that", and "that idea cannot fly" - such words bury the gifts needed to fulfill a purpose. God's people must stay away from the forces of discouragement.

Acts of Foolishness - The king's court is a place where people's gifts get developed and represent today's workplace and institutions. When people allow folly to go with them into the king's court, their gifts will never get discovered. There are numerous opportunities in the workplace where people can get equipped. Folly may manifest in the form of laziness that hinders people from getting equipped with the needed experience to exploit their gifts. They will never be helpful and just go in there to get paid and get out. They never offer to help other team members who are struggling. Some spirits lead people to misbehave when they get into the king's court. Before they got the job, they were calm-minded and honorable in their ways, after they got the job, they become lousy and lost the virtues of honor. Some get to the workplace and align with toxic people. This is another reason the Lord locks up gifts.

A Life Devoid of Research - People who do not research or ask questions will not get their gifts discovered. God has called us to ask, seek and knock. This is the only condition that allows for open doors. When life is devoid of asking questions, there is no discovery of gifts.

A Life Devoid of the Ministry of Instruction and Correction - Gifts are locked up when there is a mindset, attitude, or behavior that needs instruction or correction to be improved upon. The spirit of gifts gives room for the ministry of instruction and correction to minister to the individual. The spirit-powering gifts do not return until the ministry of instruction and correction has been fulfilled. The manifestation of this is seen daily around us; correction can be sometimes hard to receive. People leave workplaces, churches, friendships, and relationships because they are not open to correction. This is a place where gifts are locked up.

Carrying an Unassigned Burden - One of the fastest ways to lose the opportunity to discover a gift, or to get kicked out of purpose is carrying a burden (emotional, spiritual, or financial) that God forbids. Many people become burden bearers for people who have deliberately chosen a life of waste and disobedience to God. In one of our publications called "The Big Process Called Yoke", we share some revelations and definitions of yoke-breaking as a series of activities where God removes people from old processes and plants people into new processes. Many people want to live with old failures and get new successes. God does not sponsor failure.

Prayers

to Abide in God's Gifts

1. Father, thank you for the gifts you have placed in my life in the name of Jesus.
2. Father, clear away the siege of darkness against my gifts, clear away in the name of Jesus.
3. The rod of wickedness over my gifts, be shattered in the name of Jesus away.
4. Lord, the gifts are given to me that will burst me into my breakthrough, Lord, show me and activate it.
5. The gift you have given me from heaven, Lord show me, activate it, and give it unto me in the name of Jesus.
6. My natural gifts shall not expire in the name of Jesus.
7. The star of my destiny that was stolen at birth, be restored to me in Jesus name.
8. My giftings shall receive the resurrection power of the Lord in the name of Jesus.
9. Thou gift created for God's purpose in me, wake up and begin to manifest in the name of Jesus.
10. Father, multiply upon me, gifts for purpose in the name of Jesus.
11. Father, open up my eyes to see the hidden gifts you have placed in me, in the name of Jesus.
12. Father Lord, deliver me from every activity in my life that seeks to bury my gifts in the name of Jesus.
13. My Lord, deliver me from activities that seeks to chase me out of purpose in the name of Jesus.

14. Father, deliver me from forces of discouragement that seek to lock up my gifts in the name of Jesus.
15. Father, deliver me from forces of manipulation that seek to lure me out of my areas of gifts in the name of Jesus.
16. Lord, give me a mind that is open to correction, in Jesus' Name.
17. Father, activate my mind for openness in the king's court in the name of Jesus.
18. Lord, deliver me from every act of foolishness that seeks to lock me out of purpose in the name of Jesus
19. Father, deliver me from all atmospheres of closed heaven in the name of Jesus.
20. Father, open my mind to the world of research of your glory in the name of Jesus.
21. Lord Jesus, open up a deeper realm of the Word of God in me in the name of Jesus.
22. Lord, open a new realm of the Word of life in me in the name of Jesus.

Unprofaned Purpose

Journal

Chapter 8

Perfecting Gifts for God's Purpose

Perfection means no blemish is found in a thing. Perfection means having all the required and the best features ever possible. Imperfection on the other way occurs where there are impurities. Many precious metals are found in the belly of the earth and go through refinement before readiness for use. God perfects everyone He uses for His purpose. In perfecting us, He adds to us qualities, character, experiences, knowledge, and the power of the Holy Spirit to empower us to do as best as we can in a specific area in life. Gifts do not come all perfected, it needs to be refined and processed. The need for perfection arises from the need for a perfect and complete purpose of God to be fulfilled. An imperfect gift will not fulfill a perfect purpose of God and God's purpose is never imperfect. This is why the journey of perfection requires the uprooting and cutting off every non-value-adding tree in the life of a believer as Jesus taught in Matthew 7:19 - *Every tree that does not bear good fruit is cut down and thrown into the fire.* If these non-adding value elements are not cut off, purpose becomes profaned. For a good, complete, and pure purpose, gifts must be perfected. Every gift must be perfected into excellence for it to fulfill its purpose. Jesus reminds us, "Therefore you shall be perfect, just as your Father in heaven is perfect" - Matthew 5:48

Perfection of Gifts through Lens of Salvation

At the time of salvation, a believer enters a journey to perfection, having been washed by the blood of Jesus. Once that washing takes place, God leads the believer into a journey of perfection. To go on this journey, God shows the believer the true state of the believer and reveals the areas where the works of perfection need to be completed. He begins to reveal qualities, attitudes, relationships that are faulty and needing work for perfection to occur.

The Works of Perfection

The work of perfection is intense deliverance and requires committing to change of mindset, humility and openness. Here are major ways the Lord prepares us with the work of perfection.

Pruning Experiences: Consider a life that needs to resemble a beautiful tree in a beautiful garden that is well trimmed but is looking all overgrown with thorns and littered with dirt. If the tree does not return to the ideal nice looking and well-groomed state, gifts do not find the right atmosphere to thrive, and purpose is impossible to achieve. Hence, at some point, God comes with big gardening scissors to trim and reshape for beautification and conduciveness of gifts for purpose. The pruning process of any life with the Lord is never easy. Apostle Paul said he put his body to death daily. The Lord prunes when fruitfulness does not occur or has been slowed down. The Lord prunes us for growth. When we think you're all pruned and fully done, the Gardner (The Lord) comes and prunes us again.

If there are iniquities, pride, lies, malice in a life, and there's God's love for that life, He comes to prune to fulfill the Scripture: *"One who cleanses himself from these things will be a vessel for honor, sanctified, fit for the Master's use, and prepared for every good work"* - 2 Timothy 2:21. If there is hard-heartedness during the pruning process, people may get cut off from the vine.

The Furnace Experiences: Another experience that does the work of perfection is called the furnace experience. They are also called purifying experiences. These are fiery lessons of life that people go through. God uses the hotness of fire to remove impurities away from the lives of people. People who are called to fulfill God's purpose are like a sword in God's hands. When the sword gets blunt, the sword cannot function as it was meant to and requires a higher amount of force when put to use, then the sword goes through a sharpening process. There are times when the deadness of the sword will require the sword to go through fire to cut off the non-functional part and carve out new edges for precision and speed. When this is required, the sword goes through fire, it becomes liquid, and a newer shinier sword is forged out of the old one. When people go through the furnace experience, they are remodeled, and have no other choice than to shine, with no recollection of the former death, becoming more powerful and workmanship of Christ to fulfill his purpose (Ephesians 2:10).

Types of Furnace Experiences

When the Lord takes people through furnace experiences, this is usually for refinement of gifts and purification of vessels. The Scripture notes in Proverbs 27:21, *"The refining pot is for silver and the furnace for gold"*. This Scripture means that people will go through two types of furnace experiences.

The Silver Furnace Experience: The silver experience is where people get refined through lower-level teaching. Silver furnace experience is where people pass through certain degrees of training which is similar to a fiery experience. These experiences can be painful, but it teaches a good lesson and shapes people. This type of experience is usually less in magnitude compared to the gold type of furnace experience.

The Gold Furnace Experience: The gold furnace experience requires a higher degree of fire and overly hot temperature for the purifying experience to be complete. God allows certain painful fiery experiences to shape people's destinies for generations to come. The gold furnace experience is required for those who have entered a state of rottenness but carry a mighty purpose of God in them. Some people are lazy, and spoiled and will never rise to purpose until God shakes them out of their comfort zone. God uses a greater degree of fire to purify people and get them ready for an ordained purpose.

In both instances, the goal is to purify and make it ready for a purpose. The Scripture notes in Malachi 3:3 "*He will sit as a refiner and a purifier of silver; He will purify the sons of Levi, And purge them as gold and silver, That they may offer to the LORD An offering in righteousness*". The type of purifying experience is determined by the measure of unrighteousness present in peoples' lives. Once impurities are removed, the work of remodeling and destiny-reshaping begins.

Prayers

To Invite God's Perfection into Gifts and Purpose

1. Lord, I thank you for You are the God of perfection in the name of Jesus
2. Lord, let the works of your perfection go into my foundation in the name of Jesus
3. Father, let every blemish found in my life standing in the way of my gift be cleansed by the blood of Jesus.
4. Father, let every blemish in my character be taken out by the blood of Jesus.
5. Lord, you are the Creator of my destiny, I submit my life for the remodeling of my destiny in the name of Jesus.
6. Purifying fire of the Lord, purify my mind for your use and gifts in the name of Jesus
7. Purifying fire of the Lord, purify the works of my hand for to make room for your gifts and purpose in my life in the name of Jesus
8. Purifying fire of the Lord, purify my family to make room for your gifts and purpose in my life in the name of Jesus
9. Purifying fire of the Lord, purify my business to make room for your gifts and purpose in my life in the name of Jesus.
10. Purifying fire of the Lord, purify my spouse to make room for your gift and purpose in his or her life in the name of Jesus

11. Purifying fire of the Lord, purify my children to make room for your gift and purpose in my life in the name of Jesus.
12. Lord, when you have completed the works of perfection in me, do not permit me to fall into the hands of the devil, in the name of Jesus.

Journal

Chapter 9

Purpose in Time

In this chapter, we talk about one of the four components of purpose. We discussed some in the previous chapters and focus on the component of time in this chapter.

The Four Components of Purpose

Purpose carry four major components, and they are named as follows:
1. The divine agenda of God
2. The life in which it will be fulfilled
3. The location where it will be fulfilled
4. The time when it will be fulfilled.

THE AGENDA OF GOD - (What) - He will save his people from their sins - Matthew 1:21,

---

THE LIFE - (Who) - Jesus, Immanuel - Matthew 1:21, and 1:23

THE LOCATION - (Where) - But You Bethlehem, in the land of Judah, Are not the least among the rulers of Judah; For out of you shall come a Ruler Who will shepherd My people Israel - Micah 5:2

THE TIME - Then Herod, when he had secretly called the wise men, determined rom them what time the star appeared - Matthew 2:7

In our earlier chapters, we discussed some of the components. In this chapter, we discuss the timing component of purpose. The spirit of purpose lives with those who are still living. Purpose does not abide with the dead, and as a result, it is a time-sensitive spirit.

The Womb of the Morning

Psalm 110 verse 3b introduces us to the concept of the *womb of the morning*. God reveals that the morning is a segment of the day with a womb. The morning uses its womb to carry newness, procreation, life, and goodness in each day. The womb of the morning also carries the purpose for each day. The womb of the morning introduces the concept of purpose in time which is also found in Ecclesiastes 3:1 - *To everything, there is a season, A time for every purpose under heaven*: The time for preparation for purpose is the womb of the morning. The womb of the morning is defined as the morning season of people's lives which is usually marked by childhood. The womb of the morning is a season when people prepare for the purpose of their lives. The Scripture emphasizes the importance of this season of preparation and warns of the evil ahead and how to navigate through them in the book of *Job 38:12-13* saying, *"Have you commanded the morning since your days began, That it might take hold of the ends of the earth, And the wicked be shaken out of it?"*
Everyone who has come of age has gone through and out of the womb of their mornings. It was the day when children should be prepared in the ways of the Lord and speak life and goodness into the days ahead. God has given us the power to prepare for the purpose ahead by commanding the morning, as it is the foundational season of our lives.

The Three Seasons of Life

Seasons are allotted to our timeline on earth. There are three main seasons into which people's timelines can be divided.

The Morning: The morning time is the time of preparation and equipment equipped for the purpose. This is also the time of gift discovery. Gifts of children usually begin speaking for them as soon as they can speak words clearly.
    - The late morning is when a gift is fine-tuned and ready for use

The Afternoon: The afternoon season is the time when gifts have been launched;

- **Early Afternoon:** The early afternoon is when gifts are already in use and people are already working in purpose.
- **Late Afternoon:** The late afternoon is when the spirit of purpose is walking across the earth, and the glory of God that has been born forth is traveling through the ends of the earth. This occurs when people begin to discover an invention or new release from heaven, and its spreads like wildfire.

The Night: The nighttime is when an individual who has entered into purpose begins to wind down their activities to transition to the next vessel that is qualified to carry the fire of purpose into continuity.

The Levels of Time

Another division of time of life is by decades. The 2nd level of timing in a person's life is the decades. Depending on how much time a person has, it can be broken down into the following:
- Decade 1
- Decade 2
- Decade 3
- Decade 4

- Decade 5
- Decade 6
- Decade 7
- Decade 8
- Decade 9
- Decade 10
- Decade 11
- Decade 12
- and the extras

Looking at the decades above, there are just about 12 of them, and it is rare to see 120-year-olds around all the time. Analysis like this awakens us to the realities of the time in a world where the enemy seeks to steal time.

The Issachar Gift: Observation of Time

The tribe of Issachar is blessed with the gift of knowledge and observation of time. The Scriptures noted in 1 Chronicle 12:32 concerning Issachar, *"of the sons of Issachar who had an understanding of the times, to know what Israel ought to do, their chiefs were two hundred; and all their brethren were at their command".* Time is complex, but the tribe of Issachar had an understanding of time and knew what they should be doing and what purpose is to be fulfilled per time. People who walk in this anointing will have the observation of time and discovery of purpose. Such people observe the patterns of time and avoid wasting time. Anyone who fulfills purpose has mastered the principles of time, understands the calculation of times, and the patterns of time, and uses these data points to work with time.

The Elements of Time

Here are some elements of time to understand are called the window of time and the patterns of time.

The Window of Time: Time flows in a pattern. There are times that are conducive to a set of activities and there are times that are not. We were in prayers during one of our 6-Hours Worship unto Deliverance sessions, and it was a deliverance for the redemption of time. I saw a vision, there were a lot of windows all lined up, some windows were closing, and the others were opening up. I was not sure what it is, and the Holy Spirit said, these are the windows of time. Each window opens to allow people to fulfill a specific assignment for that season. I asked the Lord, when the window closes without fulfilling that assignment, what happens and the Lord says, the next window that opens to them becomes useless, and this is how people waste time.

The Pattern of Time: The pattern of time is the repeated design of the time. These are occurrences that are designed to repeat in time. This means that time has permitted only certain activities and purposes to occur at specific intervals. This is linked to the window of time. For example, a person who is looking for when to get married may find that in June of 2019 they met the one whom the Lord ordained to be their spouse, but there was a miss somewhere. Then in June of 2021, God realigns time and brings the same opportunity again, if this is a careful observer of time, they will realize there is a pattern of time. There are people who change jobs only at specific times of the year. There are people who could enter into wealth at certain times of the year. The devil also studies the pattern of time and tries to misalign people's time.

Understanding the Creation of Time

Timing can be understood when the origin of time is examined. God showed Moses some of these mysteries in Genesis 1:16, *And God said, "Let there be lights in the vault of the sky to separate the day from the night and let them serve as signs to mark sacred times, and days and years.* This moment was when the time was created into existence, with light being the framework of time. The light was made to be the marker of times, days, years, and seasons. Furthermore, God broke down time into lower levels with different degrees of light as written in Genesis 1:15-16 *and let them be lights in the vault of the sky to give light on the earth." And it was so. God made two great lights—the greater light to govern the day and the lesser light to govern the night. He also made the stars.* Following this, another low level of time is:

- Night
- Day

Those who fulfill their purpose are good managers of time, with the understanding of scheduling and being at the right place at the right time, fulfilling the right work at the right time. Without time management, gifts never get established, procrastination takes over and confusion darkens the mind. A person becomes empty when there is no proper guidance on how to use time efficiently. This is what happened at the beginning of Genesis 1: *In the beginning, God created the heavens and the earth. Now the earth was formless and empty, darkness was over the surface of the deep, and the Spirit of God was hovering over the waters. And God said, "Let there be light," and there was light. God saw that the light was good, and he separated the light from the darkness. God called the light "day," and the darkness he called "night." And there was evening, and there was morning—the first day.* The light was introduced by the Holy Spirit of God for the earth to take form, for the earth to get away from emptiness and darkness and become occupied. Also, anyone who manages time understands light. There is one power that gives that understanding, the power of the Holy Spirit.

Accounting for Time: To manage time, you need to account for time. You need to account for every time of your day. You need to break down your time into tiny bits and take note of how your mind was used at each of these times and what you produced, otherwise the devil steals your time. This is why organizations invest millions of dollars to manage time with time-tracking tools. Believers should emulate this, and properly set up accounting guidelines for their time.

Time: Planting and Harvesting Season

Timing can be looked at from the farmer's standpoint. Some crops grow faster than others. Some of the fastest-growing ones are spinach, baby carrots, lettuce, tomatoes, and other leafy vegetables. Any farmer who plants late knows that these plants can grow and be harvested within weeks. Baby carrots can be harvested in as little as 30 days and spinach is as ready in as little as 30 to 45 days. These types of plants are known as survival plants. They are the plants people can grow to feed on for survival. They grow expressly. They are the easiest crops to grow and harvest. There are some crops that take years to grow. Mango trees take between 5 to 8 years before mango can be harvested. Looking at this, a farmer who plans to harvest mangoes needs to begin planting early. In a new decade, there are 10 years. When divided into 3, we have about 3.33 years in each decade. Anyone who has missed out on entering purpose in the past decade can begin afresh in the new decade. If they approach their destiny as a plant that needs to be sown and nurtured and master the use of time, time will be redeemed, and they will be able to work in time. Anyone planting mango in the decade needs to begin in year one so they can harvest between years 5 and 8. People who are planting tomatoes have a lot of time on their side to harvest many times. Each assignment type varies, and the more powerful your purpose, the more depth you will build before you begin to harvest.

The 3-Year Rule of Rebuilding Lives

We all have our planting and harvesting season in our journey to fulfill our purpose. There is a season of sowing and planting for everyone in life. If anyone seeks to begin a new career, learn something new and get good at it, or study and become a master at a subject, there is the 3-year rule. The Scripture has a 3-year rule for people who are looking to rebuild their life to a state of stability and entry into purpose. Daniel was trained for 3 years before he could serve with the king as found in **Daniel 5:5** "*And the king appointed for them a daily provision of the king's delicacies and of the wine which he drank, and three years of training for them, so that at the end of that time they might serve before the king*".

Time and Waste

Time is a costly commodity and a prime target for satan. When satan wants to profane the purpose of individuals, he afflicts them with time wasting. He can either make people squander their time or use time wasters to usurp their time. Time wasting is one of the greatest losses that can befall people. Every time we spend living is for a purpose, if it is not fulfilled, then it is a waste of life. Many Christians go into extended spiritual war, fasting and praying to get into purpose but God is calling their attention to time management.

Some ladies complain they have been in a relationship for 6 years with their boyfriend, but he is not proposing or thinking about marriage. This is how the enemy steals people's time. Some spend 10 hours on social media, doing nothing of value, this is how the enemy wastes people's time. Agents of satan steal time by luring people with unprofitable conversations that are designed to steal time. A lady looking for deliverance from the spirit of witchcraft shared with us that she would get into the mind of people and get them to spend longer than usual hours with her using mind control. This is why a strong understanding of time will ensure that you never compromise on your time, then you will be closing the door on the enemy who seeks to steal your time.

Older people tend to appreciate time more than younger people because the value of time is revealed as we age. Parents who were once young said in their days of youth, "the future is bright". 20 years, 40 years later when they come into a time, if they are living in their God-given purpose, they testify to that, if not, they live in regret.

Time-Wasting Spirits

God created us to be relational. The plan of God was to allow people to add value to each other. However, not all relationships bring value, some relationships are channeled by which the spirit of waste thrives. The spirit powering waste works in two ways. It works from within or from without. Anytime a person nurtures waste, they attract waste to themselves. Every time given to us by the Lord is allocated toward the pursuit of a purpose. When people are in the habit of wasting time, they attract time wasters. You must be able to take account of your time, and you will always know when the spirit of waste creeps in to steal time. The devil wastes the time of many through many avenues. The spirit of waste is assigned to people to steal time, essence, virtues, and divine opportunities. The spirit of waste manifests through wasters.

Wasting Counsels: There was the woman who told us how she was prophesied to and told to marry a man. 40 years later, she realized she had married the wrong person. She had fallen into the captivity of prophets who prophesied by the wasting spirits. Those are the people who give advice that will lead to utter desolation. The demonic prophets of waste prophesy to ensure people lead a life of waste. Wasting counsels come as advice received which eventually empties people. The tool of satanic advice and suggestions has knocked many out of purpose. People who are susceptible to wasting counsel are those who go seeking various prophets to speak a word over them.

Sacrifices of Waste: There was a 78-year-old man we ministered to, he was very kind to the people around him. He said he spent all his years working, and while he worked, he spent time with his relatives, and friends, and gave them all they wanted. He was shocked that at his time of retirement, all the people he cared for had left him. This is the spirit that steals time and the rewards of time. There are relationships that are maintained with sacrifices of waste and steal the reward of time. These relationships remain only active if the ones under captivity continue to pay a ransom. Those who demand the sacrifice of waste will say, "if you do not give me this, then that would happen". The spirit invokes guilt and manipulates its victims. Many victims give out what they do not have to console the spirits. Spiritually, the spirit demands expensive sacrifices such as time, virtues, and even sometimes life from its victims. Unfortunately, anyone who submits to this spirit will be wasted. People who have no boundaries or find it difficult to say "no" to those spirits are easily held captive. This same spirit almost wasted Jehoshaphat, king of Judah who agreed to follow king Ahab to war without first inquiring from the Lord.

2 Chronicles 18: 1-4 NKJV
Jehoshaphat had riches and honor in abundance; and by marriage he allied himself with Ahab. After some years he went down to visit Ahab in Samaria; and Ahab killed sheep and oxen in abundance for him and the people who were with him, and persuaded him to go up with him to Ramoth Gilead. So Ahab king of Israel said to Jehoshaphat king of Judah, "Will you go with me against Ramoth Gilead?" And he answered him, "I am as you are, and my people as your people; we will be with you in the war." Also Jehoshaphat said to the king of Israel, "Please inquire for the word of the Lord today."

Another set of people defeated the same spirit by the wisdom of the Holy Spirit. They refused to sympathize with foolishness.
Matthew 25:1-9 NKJV

> "At that time the kingdom of heaven will be like ten virgins who took their lamps and went out to meet the bridegroom. Five of them were foolish and five were wise. The foolish ones took their lamps but did not take any oil with them. The wise ones, however, took oil in jars along with their lamps. The bridegroom was a long time in coming, and they all became drowsy and fell asleep. "At midnight the cry rang out: 'Here's the bridegroom! Come out to meet him!' "Then all the virgins woke up and trimmed their lamps. The foolish ones said to the wise, 'Give us some of your oil; our lamps are going out.'"'No,' they replied, 'there may not be enough for both us and you. Instead, go to those who sell oil and buy some for yourselves.'

The spirit of waste thrives in ungodly emotions and pity. Anyone who would conquer the spirit of waste would be the one who will not compromise on God's Word and yield to the leading of the Holy Spirit. Anyone who manages their time properly and in God's way will not fall into such problems.

Prayers

for the Redemption of Time

1. Father Lord, grant me the understanding of time, in the name of Jesus
2. Lord, deliver my times from time-wasting spirits in the name of Jesus
3. Father, let my time be fulfilled in Your will in the name of Jesus
4. Father, let my time be guarded by the power of the Holy Spirit in the name of Jesus.
5. Spirit of waste in alignment to keep my life in the cycle of waste, perish in the name of Jesus.
6. Father, wake me up to the reality of time, in the name of Jesus.
7. Oh Ancient of days, give me the understanding of times in the name of Jesus.
8. Ancient of days, order my times and seasons for your purpose in the name of Jesus.
9. The First and the Last, realign my times for your purpose in the name of Jesus.
10. Alpha and Omega, repair my foundation and restore stolen times in the name of Jesus.
11. Father, like the tribe of Issachar, give me the understanding of times and seasons in the name of Jesus.

12. Father Lord, open up my eyes to the secret of times and seasons, in the name of Jesus.
13. Father, let your light be multiplied unto me in the name of Jesus.
14. Father, empower me to use time efficiently in the name of Jesus.
15. Father, expose and destroy all time wasting activities and powers set to steal my time in the name of Jesus
16. Power wasting my life through the spirit of sympathy is destroyed in the name of Jesusin the name of Jesus
17. Powers using the spirit of sympathy to steal them from me are destroyed in the name of Jesus.
18. Negative prophecy that has been spoken into my life by the time wasting spirit is nullified in the name of Jesus.
19. Ancient covenant keepers of waste working in my foundation are destroyed by the consuming fire of the Lord in the name of Jesus.
20. Every cycle and season of waste, spoken into my future, is canceled in the name of Jesus
21. Cycles and seasons of waste spoken into my destiny are destroyed in the name of Jesus.
22. Satanic alliance with wasters in the past, present and future is consumed by the fire of the Holy Spirit in the name of Jesus.
23. Lord shine your light into every hidden area of waste in my destiny and remove all waste in the name of Jesus.
24. Lord, uproot waste from my being in the name of Jesus.
25. Give me the understanding of times in the name of Jesus
26. Father, open up new windows of time for me to fulfill the purposes I have missed in the name of Jesus
27. Father, give me the understanding of the patterns of time in the name of Jesus

Ebenezer & Abigail Gabriels

Journal

Chapter 10

Diligence as a Tool of Purpose

The toolbox of purpose is the other tools you need to fulfill a purpose. In this chapter, we look at the tool of diligence.

Diligence in the Workplace

Pilots, whether flying large airliners or tiny planes, must follow standard procedures before starting a flight. They must follow a procedure and ensure that every little detail is well taken care of. Pilots go to obtain their flight release which provides them with information such as flight route, the volume of fuel needed, flight altitude, and other information. The pilot must then go and get more information out. There are checklists for pilots to go through for minimal errors. For example, pilots are trained to check the fuel and ensure they take a look at it before take-off. This ensures the safety and eliminates the risk of flying with the wrong type of fuel or low fuel. Without following these processes, pilots endanger the lives of the masses. We can take the lessons of diligence from the pilots and apply them to our spiritual, professional, and every other area of our lives.

Understanding Diligence

Diligence is tied to purpose. There is no purpose without diligence. Diligence is Living life carefully, vigilantly, attentively, watchfully, mindfully, in absolute awareness, cautiously and under the measure. Diligence is also living life without haste and understanding that life is a marathon and not a sprint. Diligence is living a guarded lifestyle in an orderly way. Diligence means building up processes and methods to live life. Living in diligence requires examination of each event we engage with daily and following God's laid down plan as we fulfill these events. Diligence ensures we vigilantly and cautiously test the options presented before us, and follow the leading of the Holy Spirit. The Scripture says, *"Therefore, I urge you, brothers and sisters, in view of God's mercy, to offer your bodies as a living sacrifice, holy and pleasing to God—this is your true and proper worship. Do not conform to the pattern of this world, but be transformed by the renewing of your mind. Then you will be able to test and approve what God's will is—his good, pleasing and perfect will. - Romans 12:1-2*

The tool of diligence is needed to carefully examine what is presented to us, so we make decisions that lead to purpose and not away from purpose. People who lack the tool of diligence are easily misled out of purpose. Believers should seek diligence and begin to practice, and it will become a part of them. In the next chapter, we look at another tool needed to fulfill a purpose.

Prayers

for Diligence

1. Lord, visit my mind by the power of the Holy Spirit in the name of Jesus.
2. Lord, give me the gift of diligence in the name of Jesus
3. Father, rend the heaven and locate my purpose with diligence, in the name of Jesus.
4. Father, have mercy on me and restore what I have lost as a result of the lack of diligence in the name of Jesus, in the name of Jesus.
5. Lord God, forgive for the unknown times where I have thrown opportunities as a result of lack of diligence, in the name of Jesus.
6. My Father, give me the revelations of diligence that will usher me into purpose on earth in the name of Jesus.
7. My Father, release unto me the gift and spirit of diligence in all areas of my life in the name of Jesus. in the name of Jesus.
8. Lord Jesus, bring me into the perfect meeting with the opportunity for purpose, in the name of Jesus.
9. Father, I will not miss my divine opportunities in the name of Jesus.
10. Father, let your name be exalted in my life in the name of Jesus.
11. Father, let your name be glorified in my purpose in the name of Jesus.
12. Father, let your name be hallowed in my purpose in the name of Jesus.

Ebenezer & Abigail Gabriels

Journal

Chapter 11

Faith as a Tool of Purpose

Faith is required for the purpose. Faith is trusting in God's promises even when things do not look like they are happening. This section shares how faith stirs into purpose and how the lack of it can stir away from purpose. Faith in itself is the manifestation of God as "I AM" over every circumstance. Also, faith and opportunity work together, as faith requires the ability to put the opportunity to use when it is presented

How Faithlessness Hinders Purpose

Every God-given promotion will come through an opportunity. Without faith, people never take godly opportunities. During a prophetic ministry, the Lord said to tell a man who was about to get into business, "Your vehicle has been released upon you". The man said to us, "I do not even have a driver's license, and I do not have a job". God said to tell him, "Go and get ready, things do not have to go in the order of driver's license first and then job before I release a car". We told him just that. Within one week, God brought that prophecy into fulfillment. God sent a vehicle his way for him to kick off his business, but that business assignment was delayed because faith was lacking. Someone called him and said they were relocating to another state, hence they need to give their car out, and the first thought that came to their mind was the man. When he received that call, he was not prepared. He hurriedly told the person he didn't have a place to park the car. Then afterward, he remembered the prophecy and by the time he called back hours later, the person had found someone else to give the car to. Certain times, there is no faith

and that can be seen when people are no longer expecting God's word to come into fulfillment.
1. The first problem here was the lack of faith, as written in Hebrews 4:2 *For indeed the gospel was preached to us as well as to them; but the word which they heard did not profit them, not being mixed with faith in those who heard it.*
2. The second problem was the lack of preparation for the promise of God as written in *Proverbs 24:27 Put your outdoor work in order and get your fields ready; after that, build your house.*

Faith and Opportunity

Faith opens the doors of opportunities. Opportunity is one of the vehicles to purpose. However, the opportunity is a stealth vehicle, it cannot be seen with visible eyes. There is an abundance of ideas, innovators, and blessings in God's presence and people go to God in prayers to request these. God answers by giving opportunities to enter these blessings. When opportunity shows us right in front of people, people hardly identify opportunities though they have eyes, they cannot see, though they have ears, they cannot hear the loud announcements opportunity is making.

God pours out opportunities on earth, in different sizes and types, and God will always give everyone at least one opportunity to purpose. For some, the only opportunity they need to enter purpose is to repent, to do their work right, or say the right thing when they meet with the helpers of their destiny. After salvation, the greatest opportunity available to man is the opportunity of purpose, however, only a few, a very few prepare for this expensive opportunity. Many collect apparel; fine garments, sweet scents, and expensive shoes, but forget that the state of their soul will attract opportunity for the purpose them or drive away opportunity from them. Opportunities are cryptic in nature and only those who live in the spirit walk get the privilege to discover opportunity.

The Gates of Opportunity

People commit irrecoverable blunders at the gate of opportunity. The spirit of error, if allowed, gets into people who are approaching the gates of opportunity. This spirit is responsible for critical mistakes people make at important milestones in their destinies. There are a few ways this manifests. People wage war or become rude to individuals God has chosen to help their destiny. It could be a spouse God has chosen for them, but because the spouse does not look like the image in their head, they misbehave and the door of opportunity closes. People leave their roles and change their jobs before an opportunity approaches. Sometimes when people enter the gates of opportunity, the first people they look down on arrogantly are the helpers the Lord used to bring them into those higher places. Thankfully, the Spirit of purpose is a spirit of God and does not work well with the spirit of pride. This is why many people get kicked out of the arena of purpose when they fall short of the expectations of God to stay on purpose.

Prayers
for Preparation and Opportunity

1. Lord Jesus, fill me up with the spirit of faith in the name of Jesus
2. Lord Jesus, fill me up with the spirit of power in the name of Jesus.
3. Lord, Let me be prepared for you in the name of Jesus.
4. Long-lost opportunity shall be returned by the mercies of God in the name of Jesus.
5. Lord, I will not miss my divine opportunities in the name of Jesus.
6. Lord, have mercy upon me for every opportunity you have sent my way and I have trampled in the name of Jesus
7. Lord, recover all lost opportunities back to me in the name of Jesus
8. Lord my Father, open the door of opportunities in the name of Jesus
9. Father, rend the heaven and locate me with your purpose, in the name of Jesus.
10. Father, have mercy on me and restore lost opportunities in the name of Jesus, in the name of Jesus.
11. Lord God, forgive me for the unknown times when I have thrown opportunities sent my way into the garbage, in the name of Jesus.

12. My Father, give me the revelations of opportunities that will usher me into purpose on earth in the name of Jesus.

Chapter 12

People as a Tool of Purpose

People are one of the tools of purpose. People are destined to help others fulfill their purpose. If by association with Jesus, we can enjoy the benefits of salvation, then alliances are indeed powerful. The devil also seeks to place his destructive spirit in people to use people for purposes.

Anti-Purpose Alignments: Two Friends in the Workplace
Having worked with several recruiters, God continues to reveal how the devil hinders purpose through the wrong alliances. There are two friends who were roommates in school. One was smart, the other was not as smart. The smart one Mauren (not their real name) got a job. After her training on the job, she became a top performer. In the first 3 months, she started getting the attention of her managers. Mauren told Janice (her old roommate - not her real name) about her job. Janice also wanted to work at the same place. Mauren recommended Janice. The employer was pleased with Mauren's performance so far and took Janice in too. When Janice got in, Mauren's performance dropped steadily, and they formed a very toxic gang in the workplace. They became too dangerous for the organization as they were attacking every team member who outsmarted them. They were kicked out together within a month. Mauren carried God's purpose, but Janice did not. The wrong alignment kicked her out of purpose. Whenever individuals align with the wrong

people, the spirit of purpose departs.

Anti-Purpose Alignments: Romance in the Workplace

There was the case of a brother we had encountered. A married brother was praying to God for a job. He finally got a robust offer. On the day he resumed, while others were learning about the new job and seeking ways to succeed and participating in team activities healthily, the married brother became friends with a young lady at his new workplace. They swapped phone numbers, talked before and after work, and began to date secretly. He had no idea this lady was a Satanist. This new friendship opened the brother's soul to bewitchment and trapped the soul of this strange woman. The brother was called into an important business meeting at work, where he was supposed to be a major speaker. The moment the brother opened his mouth, he began to speak about the satanist. Before his 15th day at the new job, he was fired. The mission was suddenly aborted because he walked into a trap carefully set for him.

There are many people who have fallen into similar traps in the workplace, and many do not even know that such a relationship can chase them away from their purposes. Many men and women are chained to the workplace because of the unholy alliances formed in the workplaces. Whenever there is such a relationship, there is no going into purpose until it is dealt with.

The Alliance with Jonah

Jonah-type alliances are one that sinks people's purpose as seen in Jonah 1:5 & 7 ...*And they threw the cargo into the sea to lighten the ship.... Then the sailors said to each other, "Come, let us cast lots to find out who is responsible for this calamity." They cast lots and the lot fell on Jonah.* Whenever a person brings Jonah on board their life, like the sailors did, they invite losses. The sailors had to throw out their priciest possessions into the water. The story of Jonah and the sailors is a classic business lesson.

Alliances can also make or break a business. One wrong hire can crumble an entire organization. A job candidate may look in the books, but if they do not align with the purpose of the organization, the mission suffers. In the case of the sailors who were carrying goods, they had to throw off their goods in loss to calm the storm, yet the storm refused to yield because they had associated with the wrong person. Jonah's mission was different than theirs. Jonah was running away from his assignment, while they were already in their assignment. That was a mismatch, and a house divided against itself will not stand.

Jonah-like situations can defeat God's people if care is not taken. These are some of the battles that crumble the destiny of believers. The sailors carried an unauthorized person who had unsettled scores with God with them on a journey into their ship. Battles of Jonah can bring believers into desolation. Whenever a person carries a Jonah spirit along, desolation sets in. If the person escapes, they only escape with their life.

People who have Jonah-like friends find out their lives become emptied when these friendships are in place. Jonah never contributes but uses the alliance as a vehicle of transportation to their destiny. The Jonah spirit uses alliances as stepping stones to their purpose, it's never mutually beneficial. The only prayer that works is to inquire from God who Jonah is in order to identify Jonah. Once Jonah is identified, Jonah needs to be let go, otherwise, a Jonah-like battle can bring ruin and even perish, people, if care is not taken.

Alliance in Marriage

The wrong marriage casts people out of purpose. There are many who have unfortunately married the wrong spouses. When this is the situation, only the mercy of God can bring alignment into that marriage with purpose. Satan specializes in perverting purposes by matching people to the wrong spouses. This is why a lot of couples do not work together and cannot agree to on anything of purpose together.

A man who knew he was wrongfully married came for prayers because of a series of unending troubles. The Lord said, *"I am God who honors contracts, tell him to continue to pray for his wife and cannot compromise on his marriage".* We delivered the message to the man, and he did not like it. He needed a way out on time. Marriage is highly complex, and the wrong marriage brings more complexity into purpose. When there is a wrong alignment, especially when people have married wrongly, there is only one way. The only way is for the believing spouse to uncompromisingly serve God relentlessly and go deeper in humility. This is when the Lord comes through to bless with deliverance.

There are situations where believers went blindly into a marriage and they realized their spouse is a witch or in the occultic. The same Biblical principles apply. The believer seeks God earnestly and uncompromisingly.

> *But to the rest I, not the Lord, say: If any brother has a wife who does not believe, and she is willing to live with him, let him not divorce her. And a woman who has a husband who does not believe, if he is willing to live with her, let her not divorce him. For the unbelieving husband is sanctified by the wife, and the unbelieving wife is sanctified by the husband; otherwise your children would be unclean, but now they are holy. But if the unbeliever departs, let him depart; a brother or a sister is not under bondage in such cases. But God has called us to peace. For how do you know, O wife, whether you will save your husband? Or how do you know, O husband, whether you will save your wife?*
>
> **1 Corinthians 4:12-16 NKJV**

Most times, when the believers begin to take their work with the Lord more seriously, the possessed spouse will rage and attempt to stop them. Allowing yourself to be stopped is dangerous to your purpose and life. If you continue journeying deeper into God, there are only two outcomes possible: the spouse changes and surrenders to the Lord Jesus or the possessed spouse exits the marriage. We were ministering to a man of God who knew his wife was a high-ranking witch. His wife would threaten to leave the marriage whenever they attend any Church where the power of the Holy Spirit is active. She will find a spiritually dead church for them to settle her family. However, things went terribly wrong with the man and his ministry. The Lord said to remind him he was not to leave the marriage, eventually, the wife filed for divorce.

Purpose and Leaven

Purpose needs the help of people to get fulfilled. However, when people come defiled into a purpose, it becomes a threat to the entire purpose. This occurrence is seen below in the Scriptures:

> The Lord said to Joshua, "Stand up! What are you doing down on your face? Israel has sinned; they have violated my covenant, which I commanded them to keep. They have taken some of the devoted things; they have stolen, they have lied, they have put them with their own possessions. That is why the Israelites cannot stand against their enemies; they turn their backs and run because they have been made liable to destruction. I will not be with you anymore unless you destroy whatever among you is devoted to destruction.
> **Joshua 7:10-12 NIV**

Joshua, Israel's leader wondered why Israel's enemy defeated Israel. God told him something within the Israel camp is devoted to destruction. Joshua had to figure out what had brought destruction to Israel, so he began to search.

> *Then Joshua said to Achan, "My son, give glory to the Lord, the God of Israel, and honor him. Tell me what you have done; do not hide it from me." Achan replied, "It is true! I have sinned against the Lord, the God of Israel. This is what I have done: When I saw in the plunder a beautiful robe from Babylonia, two hundred shekels of silver and a bar of gold weighing fifty shekels, I coveted them and took them. They are hidden in the ground inside my tent, with the silver underneath."*
> **Joshua 7:19-20 NIV**

It turned out it was Achan who had plundered the goods of the Babylonians. God laid out the solution to this problem, in verse Joshua 7:12: <u>I will not be with you anymore unless you destroy whatever among you is devoted to destruction.</u> Achan-like situations still hold purpose. Achan-like situations can defer covenants and promises of God to people and nations for years, decades and centuries. The only type of prayer that works in Achan-like situations is inquiry prayers to figure out who the Achan is. The only lasting solution is to destroy the spirit of Achan, not physically, but spiritually. Physical alliances must also end with Achan before God's support returns.

Regardless of whether in marriage, business or in networks, whenever there is a leaven as part of a mission, the mission will not move forward. From God's Word, whenever there is corruption within a group of people, it could mean one person has gone against God's instructions, there becomes a problem, and the spirit must be destroyed.

Leaven in Business: Alliances in Teams

Many organizations are struggling to move forward in their mission because there are leavens who have found their way into those organizations. The organizations suffer the consequences of welcoming the leavens into their lumps. They penetrate the core of teams and ruin the purpose of teams. The Scripture notes in **Ecclesiastes 10:1** *"Dead flies putrefy the perfumer's ointment, And cause it to give off a foul odor; So does a little folly to one respected for wisdom and honor".*

When a team member is non-supportive of organizational goals, every one of their thoughts, words and actions will stand in opposition to the mission. God usually exposes destructive behavior for it to be fixed or removed. If left unchecked, missions will fail. As seen in the story of Achan and how deadly he was to the mission of the entire nation of Israel. There is great power in alliances for success or failure. Alliances are spiritual and can hold spiritual strongholds for the good or bad of an organization. Hence if a team member is uninterested in the success of a group, the group will struggle. This spirit shows up in teams where one person looks for ways to hold an organization back for malicious reasons.

The Power of Obedience

Obedience to God is the only way to overcome troubles that are associated with wrong alignments. The Scriptures note in Psalm 1:1 says, *Blessed is the one who does not walk in step with the wicked or stand in the way that sinners take or sit in the company of mockers.* The main point here talks about the abundance of blessings released when we align with the right people.

On marriage, God warned the Israelites in Deuteronomy 7:2-4: *and when the LORD your God delivers them before you and you defeat them, then you shall utterly destroy them. You shall make no covenant with them and show no favor to them.* "Furthermore, *you shall not intermarry with them; you shall not give your daughters to their sons, nor shall you take their daughters for your sons.* "For *they will turn your sons away from following Me to serve other gods; then the anger of the LORD will be kindled against you and He will quickly destroy you.*

Many people think they need deliverance for a spiritual

war actually do not. All they need is to follow the Word found in Proverbs 24:21, "*My son, fear the Lord and the king; Do not associate with those given to change.* The bottom line is that associations can hinder or further purpose. In marriage situations, a spouse can hinder the family's purpose. In business, one employee can hinder the mission of an organization and in ministry, one individual can wreck the ship if believers are not awakened to these mysteries.

Submission to Leadership

It is important to submit to leadership because God has given them the authority to lead into purpose. Without submitting to leadership, gifts never get discovered. Leaders are there to stir into purpose Also, many lead people wrong. Many lead people under false knowledge and authority. Many leaders lead others into ignorance and more bondage. Believers need to pray for revelation in terms of the leadership they submit to. When people submit to the wrong leadership, they lead them far away from their purpose. Many people submit to leaders who gently lead them away from God, and to themselves. This is why many Christians do not approach God themselves anymore, they believe only their pastors can speak to God for them. The purpose of God will not be fulfilled through a vessel whose activity is targeted toward the worship of another man, or idol.

People: The Right Associations

The right people can bring great success to a mission. The right people can achieve high goals. When you bring in the right people to your network or have the right partner in marriage, God's purposes will be established, and you will see results. This is why organizations spend time looking for the right individuals to become a part of their mission. The right people are God's tools of destiny. God uses the right people to build and move His purposes forward. Believers need to carefully and prayerfully select the people that will become a part of their assignments.

Prayers
for the Release of the Right People into the Arena of Destiny

1. Lord, I give you glory and honor.
2. Father, visit my life with your purifying fire in the name of Jesus
3. Father, deliver me from the company of failures in the name of Jesus
4. Father, deliver me from the association of poverty in the name of Jesus
5. Father, deliver me from the communities that lead me away from purpose in the name of Jesus.
6. Father, send my way builders of destiny in the name of Jesus
7. Father, align me with destinies you have sent me to build
   Father, align me with missions you have called me to build and advance in the name of Jesus
8. Father, remove every spirit of Achan out of my destiny in the name of Jesus
9. Lord Jesus, empower me to build others up in the name of Jesus.
10. Lord Jesus, deliver me from the powers of Jonah in the name of Jesus.
11. Father, let your spirit of obedience rise up in me in the name of Jesus
12. Father, plant me amongst the people that will further your purpose on earth in the name of Jesus.

13. Father, rend the heaven and break me free from every alliance ruining my life, in the name of Jesus.
14. Father, have mercy on me and deliver me from alliances that oppose your purpose for me, in the name of Jesus.
15. Lord God, erect a wall of separation between myself and every purpose killer that I have aligned with, in the name of Jesus.
16. My Father, deliver me from associations that are unprofitable to my soul, in the name of Jesus.
17. My Father, deliver me from alliances that are unprofitable to my purpose, in the name of Jesus.
18. Lord Jesus, scatter every satanic alliance against my purpose, in the name of Jesus.
19. Father, destroy all alliances forming to hinder me from entering into purpose in the name of Jesus.
20. Father, set me free from alliances that divert away from purpose in the name of Jesus.
21. Father, unveil every satanic agent assigned to harvest my soul in the name of Jesus.
22. Father, expose and destroy the powers of Judas planning to mortgage my purpose to the highest bidder in the name of Jesus.
23. Father, let my life and purpose be surrounded by the fire of the Holy Spirit, and let every satanic agent assigned to me from the pit of hell, be consumed in the fire of the Holy Ghost in the name of Jesus.
24. The powers of purpose abusers are destroyed in the name of Jesus.
25. Powers of Ahithophel, sitting by the gate of my purpose, are consumed by the fire of the Holy Spirit, in the name of Jesus.

Ebenezer & Abigail Gabriels

Journal

Chapter 13

Excellence as a Tool for Purpose

The Spirit of Purpose can be explained as a Spirit of God dwelling in the core of God's presence. Anyone who wishes to enter purpose must go through many gates - one of those gates is the gate of excellence. There is no entrance into purpose if the threshold of excellence is not met. Hence, mediocrity is the enemy of purpose. The Spirit of Purpose runs far from those who live a life of mediocrity.

Excellence: An Attribute of God

Excellence surpasses ordinary standards. It means the very best. The best amongst the best. Excellence is a trait of God: In describing His Excellency, He introduces Himself as the King of kings and the Lord of lords. The Scripture further reveals that anyone associated with God also carries His excellence. This is said of Jesus Christ, the Firstborn, the Son of the Highest God is placed in the place and position of excellence. We are also told about the excellent name of Jesus

> *Therefore God also has highly exalted Him and given Him the name which is above every name, that at the name of Jesus every knee should bow, of those in heaven, and of those on earth, and of those under the earth, and that every tongue should confess that Jesus Christ is Lord, to the glory of God the Father. He has given Him a name above all names: the name of Jesus.*
> **Philippians 2:9- 10 NKJV**

God has a reputation of making anyone aligned with him carry His trait of excellence. The Spirit of Purpose only resides in people living in excellence. Believers must go all the way into the realm of excellence. It is not appropriate for a person who is described as the Son of the Highest God not to be associated with excellence. Moses walked in excellence. He excelled so much that God said to Him, "*See, I have made you as a God to Pharaoh, and Aaron your brother shall be your prophet*" - Exodus 7:1.

The Firstborn Mystery

The Spirit of Excellence precedes the Spirit of Purpose. The Spirit of Excellence is reflected in the divine rights of the firstborn. God said in *Psalm 89:27 said*, "*I also shall make him My firstborn, The highest of the kings of the earth.* By God's design, firstborns are ordained into excellence. The ideal image of the first child is to have spiritual maturity, authority over the younger ones, leaders of siblings, leadership over younger children, and keepers of the younger ones. This is seen in the event described in *Hebrews 1:6: And when He again brings the firstborn into the world, He says, "and let all the angels of God worship Him"* When God had all His other creations bow to Jesus.

The Spirit of excellence has however been lost by many who are positioned as first child in the family, because of the curse of Esau.

Genesis 25:31-34 NKJV

"*But Jacob said, "Sell me your birthright as of this day." And Esau said, "Look, I am about to die; so what is this birthright to me?" Then Jacob said, "Swear to me as of this day." So he swore to him, and sold his birthright to Jacob. And Jacob gave Esau bread and stew of lentils; then he ate and drank, arose, and went his way. Thus Esau despised his birthright.*"

Esau had no idea who he was or what the privileges of the firstborn are. He had no revelation, and he sold out all of the rights of the firstborn. The Scripture warned in Hebrews 12:16 -- *that there be no immoral or godless person like Esau, who sold his birthright for a single meal.*

Firstborn and Excellence
There is a spiritual association between people who fall into the category "firstborns" of their parents and the "spirit of excellence". Genesis 49:3-4 *"Reuben, you are my firstborn; My might and the beginning of my strength, Preeminent in dignity and preeminent in power. Uncontrolled as water, you shall not have the preeminence (you shall not excel), Because you went up to your father's bed; Then you defiled it--he went up to my couch.* The place of a firstborn is a powerful one, and there is a curse that seeks to hinder the excelling of firstborns.

> **1 Chronicles 5:1-2**
> *Now the sons of Reuben the firstborn of Israel (for he was the firstborn, but because he defiled his father's bed, his birthright was given to the sons of Joseph the son of Israel; so that he is not enrolled in the genealogy according to the birthright. Though Judah prevailed over his brothers, and from him came the leader, yet the birthright belonged to Joseph),*

The curse of the firstborn is the anti-excellence curse which began from Adam, he was the first creation, and lost his place over a taste of the forbidden fruit. This curse rolled over till it got to Esau and then Reuben. Reuben was supposed to showcase the image of his father. He was supposed to manifest the dignity, strength, and power of his father, just like Jesus is the glory of the Father and a reflection of Him. One who finds themselves in the firstborn position needs to prayerfully contend to hold on to excellence and get into purpose.

The Spirit of Excellence and the Curse of Reuben

The curse of Reuben is bluntly against the spirit of excellence. When the Reuben-like curse is at work in the life of a person, the spirit of excellence never rests on that person. A person may be subject to the curse of the Reuben if they were the first child of their parents and they have not sought the Lord in prayer to break the occurrence of this curse over their lives and their descendants. They may find it hard to excel or maintain excellence. They may fall short in everything while other siblings excel.

The spirit of excellence does not stay when there is defilement in the life of a person. All works of iniquity bring defilement. Sexual sin, talkativeness, indiscipline, corruption, alignment with the wrong people, idol worship, involvement with witchcraft, contact with cursed objects, incest, and all other forms of ungodliness. Where all these are, the spirit of excellence goes far away from there. One major spirit that locks people out of purpose is the spirit of mediocrity. The absence of the spirit of excellence is a curse. This curse is very potent, it tears the kingdom away from the one who is supposed to be the leader and gives the kingdom to others.

Priesthood and ministry are impossible where this curse is at work. Anyone living under the curse of Ruben cannot make a mark or serve their purpose in life. The voice of the curse in their foundation speaks against them and is constantly demanding a ransom of constant failure. The spirit responsible for sponsoring the lack of excellence is the spirit of mediocrity.

Mediocrity ruins purposes, and God's people must stay away from every appearance of mediocrity to advance their purposes. When a person observes that excellence is not found in their lives; it's time to zealously seek deliverance in that area, so that they may be set free and that the spirit of excellence may return.

Excellence Habits and Lifestyles

Not all cases of the lack of excellence are spiritual in nature. There are lifestyles that do not support excellence. Where you see mediocrity, inferiority, deficiency, inadequacy, lowliness, faults, and disvalue, excellence is not close by. People can tell they are not excelling when there's hard work but little rewards, instability, and being tossed to and from one job to the other without advancing, these are indicators that life is not excelling. Where there's no excellence, the absence of excellence is usually visible in multiple areas: marriage, family, career, spirituality, speech, love, understanding, and thoughts. No one can enter into purpose without carrying the excellency of God's power and as a result, all habits that prohibit excellence must be cut short.

Prayers

of Deliverance from the Curse Hindering Excellence

1. Father, shine the light of your gospel into my foundations in the name of Jesus.
2. Father, deliver me from the curse of "thou shall not excel" that is at work in my life, in the name of Jesus.
3. Father, empower me to carry the excellence of your power, in the name of Jesus.
4. Lord, chase out the spirit of mediocrity away from me in the name of Jesus
5. My Father, restore unto me the excellence of your glory in the name of Jesus.
6. Father, turn my life away completely from mediocrity in the name of Jesus.
7. My Father, let the spirit of excellence dwell with me in the name of Jesus.
8. My Father, deliver me from the spirit that drags into mediocrity in the name of Jesus.
9. My Father, deliver me from associations that drags into mediocrity in the name of Jesus.
10. My Father, break me completely from the curse of Reuben by your unending and tender mercies in the name of Jesus.
11. My Father, kill every habit and lifestyle that fosters mediocrity in the name of Jesus.
12. Father, let me be known by your name called "Excellence" in the name of Jesus.

Journal

Chapter 14

Journaling as a Tool for Purpose

People who journal are more likely to fulfill their purpose than those who do not. From the previous chapters, it is obvious the nature of purpose is complex. The revelation of purpose is released in bits by season. Throughout our lifetime here on earth, God continues to release information about our purpose till it is fulfilled and we go home to be with the Lord. Hence, revelation is required every step of the way for a believer to fulfill their purpose on earth. The difference between the one who journals and the one who does not is that one has captured the voice and the words of God which brings vision and understanding to them, and the other has not captured the vision, thereby becoming confused.

The Lord entrusts information into the trusted hands of those who journal because they are diligent keepers of history. Journaling preserves the history and helps further God's purpose across generations.

The Prophetic Nature of Written Words

Writing inspired by the Holy Spirit encodes mysteries and prophecies. Many writers are prophets, and many prophets are writers. Many prophets of the Bible were writers - Moses, David, ,Ezrah, Nehemiah, Moses, Isaiah, Jeremiah, Daniel, Hosea, Joel, Amos, Obadiah, Jonah, Micah and others. Many disciples were writers - Paul, Peter, John, Jude, James, Luke, John Mark, and Matthew were all writers.

> *"Write the vision,*
> *And make it plain on tablets,*
> *That he may run who reads it.*
> *For the vision is yet for an appointed time;*
> *But at the end it will speak, and it will not lie.*
> *though it tarries, wait for it;*
> *Because it will surely come, It will not tarry.*
> **Habbakuk 2:2-3 NKJV**

When believers write down the words coming to mind, they are downloading and recording information from heaven. This information is sent to the believer because the plans communicated are needed on earth. When we write, we store information, and that information can be used to implement divine strategies. When it is not written that new knowledge does not come through the earth to resolve problems where needed.

Why the Devil Hates Journaling

Journaling brings light and clarity, it destroys darkness. It reminds us of ideas received. Those who journal will hardly become confused. Satan sends his agents all around the world to distribute confusion into people's minds. He seeks to bring doubt and get people to start thinking, *"did I truly hear from the Lord"*? *"did I hear God say clearly, or was it me thinking God said when God didn't say"*. The devil hates journaling because those who journal are more likely to revisit information given to them and work under the guidelines of the information than those who did not. This is why the first point of attack on the woman in the Garden of Eden was to fire an arrow of doubt at the instructions God had given to Adam. The devil asked, "Has God indeed said, 'You shall not eat of every tree of the garden'?" in Genesis 3:1. If Eve had written down or had access to a written down instruction, she might have acted differently. The devil hates journaling and seeks to underestimate it or get people thinking their brains can retain information. It is a ploy of the devil, to discourage from capturing powerful and destiny-helping ideas and secrets from God.

The Value of Information

Money cannot purchase valuable information. Heavenly information is one of the rare privileges enjoyed by the believer. Here on earth, there is tons of information but the relevant information for purpose is scarce. There is a special policy of the kingdom of God, and it is the sealing of information. Information is costly, and this is why God seals information, so it is not abused. Jesus informed His disciples in *Matthew 13:11 - He replied, "The knowledge of the mysteries of the kingdom of heaven has been given to you, but not to them.*

Information Medium

God speaks to people through many mediums: Dreams, visions, Words of the Scripture, prophets, inspiration, ideas dropped in their minds, spirit-filled music, godly books, symbols, heavenly bodies, and elements (stars, rain, the earth, etc). The wise men who went to worship Jesus read the signs and were led to the location of the baby by the star of Jesus.

Signals through the Elements: There was a revival breakout during one of the Bible Studies at Lighthill Church in 2018. We went for a 1-hour Bible Study, which lasted for about 9 hours, and continued for the next 7 days. We all enjoyed the Presence of the Word amongst us over the next 6 days. People came after work, including those finishing work around midnight to join the continued Bible discussion each day every day and we would all leave around 3am-4am each morning. This was uncommon in America, especially since people have very tight work schedules. This means that most times every program needs to be scheduled. However, during this revival breakout which wasn't planned, people showed up for 7 days. All 7 days it rained, and by the 7th day, we discovered it was the seven days leading to Rosh Hashanah - the Jewish New Year. This was God speaking to us through the signs of the rain.

Information through Dream: God speaks by dreams. Joseph the husband of Mary (mother of Jesus) received major instructions through dreams. The Scripture notes in Matthew 2:13, *"Now when they had departed, behold, an angel of the Lord appeared to Joseph in a dream, saying, "Arise, take the young Child and His mother, flee to Egypt, and stay there until I bring you word; for Herod will seek the young Child to destroy Him."* The Lord speaks to people majorly through the dreams, unfortunately, the devil has created and circulated the following phrases: *"it was just a dream"*, *"it was a nightmare"*, *"dreams are sometimes foolish"*, *"dreams are superstitions"*. The goal is to get you to discount and dump the information given in the dream in the trash.

Agents of darkness have mastered how to manipulate dreams. This is why people need to be careful who they share their dreams with. There was an individual who led a ministry and was working in witchcraft. She kept asking people, "what dreams did you have?". When they tell her the dreams, she misleads them with the wrong interpretation. Many people's purpose has been destroyed as a result.

The Treasures of the Written Words

We usually tell people to keep a dream journal, and the Lord will make a way for interpretation. Written words are assets needed for a purpose. The lack of it is a liability. One of the reasons why Israel is cherished by God is that they keep history and pass it to upcoming generations.

> *Tell it to your children, and let your children tell it to their children, and their children to the next generation*

Joel 1:3 NKJV

The Scripture above reveals that Israel was instructed to tell their upcoming generations about the ways and their relationship with the Lord so that they can keep, for this reason, they have kept the word of God and are careful to observe His ordinances and principles. When we write, we remember the words spoken by the Lord and we go ahead and live by those words. Those who do not journal are prone to mistakes, and they live an error-prone life which consumes a lot of their time. To rise above confusion and for clarity, journaling is a key requirement to fulfilling the purpose.

Prayers

for the Power to Retain & Execute the Revelation of Purpose through Journaling

1. Lord, I thank you for your revelation in the name of Jesus.
2. Father, open the mysteries of journaling to me in the name of Jesus.
3. Release to me the power to write down your ideas for me in the name of Jesus.
4. My Father, sensitize and empower me to write down heavenly visions to be fulfilled on earth
5. My Father, empower me to write down assignments given me from heaven as you show me in the name of Jesus.
6. Lord my God, open the book you wrote concerning me unto me in the name of Jesus.
7. Lord, let me capture the deep things you're revealing to me in the name of Jesus.
8. Lord Father, no longer will confusion know my life in the name of Jesus
9. Lord Jesus, through the power of capturing down the words you speak unto me, let darkness clear away from my life in the name of Jesus.
10. No longer will the enemy enroll me in his playbook in the name of Jesus.
11. Let heavenly resources be released unto me in the name of Jesus.

Ebenezer & Abigail Gabriels

Journal

Chapter 15

Promotion as a Tool for Purpose

When you think about purpose, think of promotion as a location. Anna founded a fashion company. Anna hired new employees and one of the employees she hired was a Sales Manager called Joshua. Joshua just graduated and he studied Electronics at the University. All through Joshua's childhood, he had a dream of becoming an electrician and God had given Him different revelations confirming his dreams. He innovated new devices, never-seen-before, and everyone was fascinated by how a little kid came up with such creativity. After completing his Bachelor of Science, he was hoping to start his electrical engineering business but was not sure how to raise funds. He found an opportunity at Annas Company and helped supervise the electrical unit. Very soon, Joshua discovered that salespeople who got in large contracts were earning big commissions. He switched to sales and performed well. His plans of innovating new electrical devices soon began to fade away as he was overtaken by the commissions and the promotions he was getting in the workplace. In Joshua's situation, his purpose was to invent new electrical devices, and his promotion in the pathway of a salesman continues to lead him away from the location.

Promotion is a location in the pathway of purpose, intended to bring people closer to their purpose. When we see promotion as a location, then we ask if our current promotion leads us closer or far away from our purpose.

Types of Promotions

There are three main types of promotion discussed in this section namely:

1. False Promotions
2. Pre-offers
3. True Promotions

False Promotions: Some promotions are called *false promotions*. False promotion leads people far away from the purpose of God. False promotion is one of the tools of the devil used to distract people out of God's purpose. *Proverbs 3:35 says The wise shall inherit glory: but shame shall be the promotion of fools.* False promotion is a grand scheme and a tool of diversion off the course of purpose. False promotion locks people out of purpose and has brought death in some situations. This was the situation for Naboth who refused to sell his vineyard.

> *He answered her, "Because I said to Naboth the Jezreelite, 'Sell me your vineyard; or if you prefer, I will give you another vineyard in its place.' But he said, 'I will not give you my vineyard.'" Jezebel his wife said, "Is this how you act as king over Israel? Get up and eat! Cheer up. I'll get you the vineyard of Naboth the Jezreelite." So she wrote letters in Ahab's name, placed his seal on them, and sent them to the elders and nobles who lived in Naboth's city with him. In those letters she wrote: "Proclaim a day of fasting and seat Naboth in a prominent place among the people. But seat two scoundrels opposite him and have them bring charges that he has cursed both God and the king. Then take him out and stone him to death."*

1 King 21:6-10NKJV

Naboth was deceived into false promotion. If he knew it was a false promotion, he would not have honored the invite. To Naboth, it seemed like an invitation into royalty, but it was a call into untimely death. If Naboth had the spirit of discernment, he would not die untimely. This is why not every invitation, or promotion is indeed a promotion. False promotions also come into a place where people neglect the words of Psalm 75:6-7 which says - *For exaltation comes neither from the east, Nor from the west nor from the south. But God is the Judge: He puts down one, And exalts another.* When the promotion is sourced by an individual themselves outside of the will of God, such promotion, if obtained, does not lead to God's purpose.

The devil uses the tool of false promotion. He deceived Adam and Eve into false promotion, telling the woman they would be promoted into a place of discernment and enlightenment. Their fall into the deceit of false promotion led to their death.

Pre-Offers: Pre-offer precedes God's promotions. They are offers that look like real promotions, but it is a false offer to lure away from the upcoming promotions from God. Some try to use pre-offers as a stepping stone into the promotion. The problem with pre-offer is that people may dwell in this longer than they are supposed to and that they slumber when true promotion comes. Some pre-offers are not to be accepted because they may be presented to lead away from God's purpose. Pre-offer usually looks very attractive and can only be caught by the Spirit of God. When people are praying to find their spouse, a pre-offer may come first, God's people must be able to detect it by the power of the Holy Spirit.

True Promotions: These are promotions sanctioned by the Lord. They are intended to lead toward purpose. All true promotions come from God. This is why the Scriptures record:

He also chose David His servant, And took him from the

sheepfolds; From following the ewes that had young He brought him, To shepherd Jacob His people, And Israel His inheritance.So he shepherded them according to the integrity of his heart, And guided them by the skillfulness of his hands.
Psalm 78:70-72 NKJV

God is the One who promotes. God's promotions are true and real. God promotes the most unlikely situations after hard work and obedience. There is no promotion that comes without hard work David's story was one of God's true and unending promotions. David was content with his role as a keeper of sheep, and when God found him faithful, God visited David and promoted him. To date, God continues to promote worshippers - descendants of David who walk in the ways of the Lord.

Using the Tool of Discernment to Destroy False Promotion Discernment

True promotion is concealed by the Lord. Hence, it is quite difficult to discern. Prophet Samuel could not easily discern whom the Lord had promoted in the house of Jesse. The prophet Samuel was a national prophet as well as a Judge of Israel. Yet, he could not easily discern the one to anoint. If promotion was easy to identify, Samuel would have asked for David immediately after he got to the house of Jesse. The verses below tell about the encounter of Samuel on the day he went to figure out the One whom the Lord had promoted.

"And he said, "Peaceably; I have come to sacrifice to the Lord. Sanctify yourselves, and come with me to the sacrifice." Then he consecrated Jesse and his sons, and invited them to the sacrifice. So it was, when they came, that he looked at Eliab and said, "Surely the Lord's anointed is before Him!" But the Lord said to Samuel, "Do not look at his appearance or at his physical stature, because I have refused him. For the Lord does not see as man sees; for man looks at the outward appearance, but the Lord looks at the heart." So Jesse called Abinadab, and made him pass before Samuel. And he

> said, "Neither has the Lord chosen this one." Then Jesse made Shammah pass by. And he said, "Neither has the Lord chosen this one." Thus Jesse made seven of his sons pass before Samuel. And Samuel said to Jesse, "The Lord has not chosen these." And Samuel said to Jesse, "Are all the young men here?" Then he said, "There remains yet the youngest, and there he is, keeping the sheep." And Samuel said to Jesse, "Send and bring him. For we will not sit down till he comes here." So he sent and brought him in. Now he was ruddy, with bright eyes, and good-looking. And the Lord said, "Arise, anoint him; for this is the one!" Then Samuel took the horn of oil and anointed him in the midst of his brothers; and the Spirit of the Lord came upon David from that day forward. So Samuel arose and went to Ramah".
> **1 Samuel 16:5-13NKJV**

Samuel, an experienced prophetic national leader, had almost explored all the options placed before him. Yet, He kept hearing God saying "No" to the candidates presented for promotion. After all the options had been exhausted, Samuel asked, "*Are all the young men here?*". It was then that David was brought from the sheepfold. If Samuel almost missed the chosen one to be promoted, anyone could miss it. Samuel could have missed it all if He hadn't learned to hear from God or if he didn't check with God through every choice that was presented to him. If Samuel had missed it, the long-term effect of bringing the wrong person into the place of David would have ruined God's purpose for Israel until Israel got back on track. Promotion is concealed, and the first response when there is a perceived call into promotion is to go into God's presence for clarifications.

Discernment is your major tool you'll need to avoid a fall into false promotion, pre-offers. Discernment is also the guide into true promotion.

> But solid food belongs to those who are of full age, that is, those who by reason of use have their senses exercised to discern both good and evil.
> **Hebrews 5:14 NKJV**

God wants us to become mature and be able to distinguish between what is good and bad for purpose. God wants His people to tell whether a promotion is false or true. Godly promotions usually do not follow a common pattern. Godly promotions usually come out of faithful and diligent living.

Prayers
for the Entry into God's Promotion

1. Lord, baptize me with the spirit of discernment in the name of Jesus.
2. My Father, open my eyes into the secrets of promotion in the name of Jesus.
3. My Father, show me the promotions aligned for me in the name of Jesus
4. Father Lord, bring me out of every false promotion in the name of Jesus.
5. Father, give me an understanding of what false promotion is, in the name of Jesus.
6. Father, expose every pre-offer of darkness designed to lure me out of purpose, in the name of Jesus
7. Promotion of darkness, place before me to deter me from purpose, be exposed and destroyed by the power in the name of Jesus.
8. Father open my senses for discernment in the name of Jesus
9. Lord, I will not miss my true promotions in the name of Jesus
10. Lord Jesus, open my eyes to recognize your true promotions for me in the name of Jesus.
11. Lord of glory, my true promotions will not be traded for false promotions and pre-offers in the name of Jesus.
12. Lord Jesus, promote me into purpose.

Ebenezer & Abigail Gabriels

Journal

Chapter 16

The Retreat of Destiny and Discovery of Purpose

Remember at the beginning, we told you the book Unprofaned Purpose will not show you 10 ways to become rich, or 20 steps to becoming successful, but will bring you into a lot of powerful revelations on purpose. Many people have missed their purposes for many reasons including the misuse and misunderstanding of the soul, tools of the time, diligence, alliances, natural gifts, journaling, and promotion but to mention a few. Now, you have found knowledge, your soul is beckoned to take the spiritual retreat of your life where you will commune with the Lord Jesus, who will give you the blueprint of your life as it is in Heaven. You will be taken on a journey where the Lord will show you your life's design at the moment of your creation which you are to re-live on earth.

Once in a lifetime, a retreat of purpose is needed by anyone who dares to fight for their purpose in life. You will learn why from the story of the perforated pot.

The Perforated Pot

In ancient times, African mothers who double as home managers paid special attention to their cookware. Many of their cooking vessels had a long-life span. A lot of them used a few sets of cooking pots throughout their entire marital life. Their cookware was their most precious possession. Some of this cookware was made of aluminum. It meant a lot to them. Some were wedding gifts passed to them by their mothers. Some were products of their hard-earned money from their numerous petty trades. The pots were pricier to them also because they represented the container that housed the food of the entire family - day and night in the times when there were no refrigerators or microwaves. Once a hole was found in a pot - the mother's heart breaks. She understands that her food holder is perforated and can no longer hold food on or off the fire. She swiftly looks for a porter skilled in pottery repair to mend and prepare it for subsequent uses. Those mothers treated their pots with care because they understood the values that were attached to those pots.

Like the perforated pot, the one who lives without the knowledge of the reason for their existence is a person whose life is perforated on many sides. These perforated areas are the entrance points for profanity into their lives. They are also the points where their destiny is being sieved away. Although life may initially appear to be filled with interesting activities which excite them - these are mere fillers placed into the spacious areas of their lives to hold up those places. When closely examined, the fillers yield nothingness in place of fulfillment of destiny. A perforated life is filled with the darkness and leakage of virtues. A life outside of the knowledge of one's purpose absorbs one into confusion.

Why We Exist

Mankind is on earth for two purposes and the first purpose is the building unit of the second purpose.

Purpose 1 ⇢ DISCOVERY
Purpose 2 ⇢ THE GRAND PURPOSE

Purpose 1: Discovery

Discovery is the journey we take to search out the reason why we were created. It is our journey to a place of destiny discovery. The reason why we communicated that *Unprofaned Purpose* will not show you step-by-step plans to become rich or get is that the very first purpose is "to discover".

A discovery mission is usually very difficult to fulfill. Many become weary and fall off the mission, resorting to a life that was never designed for them.

> *I, the Preacher, was king over Israel in Jerusalem. And I set my heart to seek and search out by wisdom concerning all that is done under heaven; this burdensome task God has given to the sons of man, by which they may be exercised.*
> **Ecclesiastes 1:12 & 13 NKJV**

Solomon informs us ahead of the weighty responsibility involved in searching out our purpose.

Knowing that at birth, our life does not come with a printed manual. There is a tendency for errors and every error leads farther away from the purpose and lack of clarity of purpose. This is why there is a need for a treat of purpose.

A retreat of purpose is needed by those who are yet to discover their main assignment in life and those whose destinies have been perforated with holes and thereby leaking virtues. During this retreat is where all the holes causing leakages of all the goodness of the Lord deposited in them must be completely closed. This discovery journey is called *the Retreat into Destiny*.

The Retreat into Destiny

The *Retreat into Destiny* is where you have a resolve to walk into your original purpose in life in a timely manner. During a *Retreat of Destiny*, you are asking God to redeem your time, and willing to give all to fulfill His purpose while you are still here on earth. You are asking the Lord to activate the Spirit of Purpose for the missions ahead. A decision to take a retreat into destiny is a tough-life decision. Many people are not aware of the existence of such retreats, only a few are aware. Out of the few that are aware, only a tiny portion will ever reach a final settlement to go into one. The enemy fights people hard to prevent this retreat from taking place.

Restriction For Access

A person who is determined to search out their assignment in life is like entering into a highly restricted area for access to God's presence. The place where access is granted to those who walk in their purpose is a very restricted place of discipline. This place is the incubation of destiny. It is a place where heaven's instructions for purpose become clearer to people. It is a place where noise is not allowed.

The Number of Access: 40-day Fast Access Code

40! Forty! F O R T Y is the number required to get complete access and entry into the revelation of purpose from God's presence. A 40-day spent in worship, fasting and prayer is the access code. For a complete transformation of a destiny, 40 days is the key to the retreat of renewal of life to enter purpose. It was no coincidence that Jesus went on into the wilderness for 40 days and 40 nights. When Jesus was born, the announcement of His birth was made. He lived normally until he was led into the wilderness by the Holy Spirit. However, a time came when God needed to transform Him from being a man into an anointed man of power. We are reminded of this event Acts 10:38 *how God anointed Jesus of Nazareth with the Holy Spirit and with power, who went about doing good and healing all who were oppressed by the devil, for God was with Him.* When people begin to search for their purpose, the Holy Spirit beckons on people onto the 40-day fasting journey for a process of the crucifixion of the flesh where the spiritual eyes are opened, and spiritual senses heightened.

This is a type of spiritual exercise you do not need to seek approval because it is the fight for your destiny. This same access is the same one that Jesus had to receive before he could enter 40 days before His ministry began on earth. 40 is the number of days for a person to continue to ask the Lord in prayers for a retreat of renewal, for the realignment of destiny, and for clarity of purpose. It is a wilderness experience. These 40 days of continuous fasting and prayer will open the door of revelation into the destiny of mankind. Inside the door of revelation, a library room filled with stacks of scrolls containing information for every season in people's life leading to the fulfillment of a grand purpose.

In the journey of discovery, we are often led to a place of segregation, a place where the voice of the Lord brings clarity. In this journey, there will be a lot of cutting off, shedding off baggage, letting go of worthless physicians, uprooting old destructive behavior, and being replanted. At the end of the retreat is a new life of power, a buildup of spiritual power and spiritual vitality for strength to reach a place where we are no longer blind to our grand purpose; where our spirit rules over the flesh, and where life is re-aligned to God's agenda.

Purpose 2: Grand Discovery

Man's grand purpose is to worship the Lord. Man's grand purpose is to complete all assignments given by the Lord and still be found admissible into Heaven to reign with Jesus forever. Our grand purpose is our specific area of ministry on earth which must be discovered, explored, and developed to show forth God's glory. Some are like Jeremiah sent to uproot evil out of foundations and replant, Moses was sent to deliver out of captivity, give laws, and lead into a new place, Noah was sent to deliver the righteous from peril and the Apostles were sent to spread the gospel to the ends of the earth. Every leader is sent to fulfill a specific purpose of God at some point. What an honor to be called to fulfill God's purpose. If we realize that each step we take brings us closer or farther away from our grand purpose, we live life in measure, and in the awe of God. Take a cue from the parables of the trees:

> *"Once the trees went out to anoint a king over themselves. So they said to the olive tree, 'Be our king!' "But the olive tree replied to them, 'Should I stop producing my oil, which is how gods and humans are honored, so that I can go to sway over the trees?' "So the trees said to the fig tree, 'You come and be king over us!' "The fig tree replied to them, 'Should I stop producing my sweetness and my delicious fruit, so that I can go to sway over the trees?' "Then the trees said to the vine, 'You come and be king over us!' "But the vine replied to them, 'Should I stop providing my wine that makes gods and humans happy, so that I can go to sway over the trees?' "Finally, all the trees said to the thornbush, 'You come and be king over us!' "And the thornbush replied to the trees, 'If you're acting faithfully in anointing me king over you, come and take shelter in my shade; but if not, let fire come out of the thornbush and burn up the cedars of Lebanon.'"*
> **Judges 9:8-15 CEB**

The fig tree understood its purpose, which is to worship God by producing sweetness and delicious fruits. Each of us has been given a specific purpose to delight God, and we must let go of every other lower calling that seeks to knock us out of God's greatest call, which is to worship Him through the fulfillment of the purpose He placed in our care.

The journey into purpose as you now know begins with a Retreat of Destiny, and that retreat begins with a contrite heart, a fast, and the question: Thou God of Purpose, What is my Purpose on Earth?

Prayers

The Prayer of Purpose

1. Father, let the Spirit of Purpose rise up concerning my life in the name of Jesus.
2. Father, let me encounter purpose as I did on the day You created me in the name of Jesus.
3. Father, let my voice begin to align with the voice of purpose in the name of Jesus.
4. Father, open unto me your purpose for my life, in the name of Jesus.
5. Father, open up the path into my purpose, in the name of Jesus
6. Father, take me from spiritual mediocrity to spiritual excellence, in the name of Jesus.
7. Release unto me divine revelation for purpose in the name of Jesus.
8. Father, have mercy upon me in the name of Jesus, so I can fulfill the purpose you have made me for in the name of Jesus.
9. Father, let me not be a vessel unto waste in the name of Jesus.
10. Lord, let me know be a useless vessel unto you in the name of Jesus.
11. Father, let me be a vessel unto honor in the name of Jesus.
12. Father, uproot my life from every activity that is distracting me from purpose in the name of Jesus
13. Father, uproot my life from every association that is toxic to my purpose in the name of Jesus

14. Father, let my purpose roar forth in the name of Jesus
15. Father, redeem my time for purpose in the name of Jesus
16. Father, realign time for me to fulfill my purpose in the name of Jesus
17. Father, send me helpers of destiny that will help me build in the assignment of purpose in the name of Jesus
18. Father, defend your interest over my life as a vessel carrying you repurpose in the name of Jesus
19. Father, let my body support my purpose in the name of Jesus
20. My spouse shall walk in their purpose in the name of Jesus
21. My children shall walk in their purpose in the name of Jesus
22. Lord, at the end of my time on earth, let not the purpose fulfilled in me suffer corruption in the name of Jesus

Unprofaned Purpose

Journal

ABOUT THE AUTHORS

Ebenezer Gabriels is an Innovator, Apostle of the Lord Jesus, the Apostle of Worship, Innovation Leader, Prophetic Leader, Revivalist, and a Computer Scientist who has brought heaven's solutions into Financial markets, Technology, and Government with his computational gifts. Apostle Gabriels is anointed as a Prophetic Leader of nations with the mantle of healing, worship music, national deliverance, foundational deliverance, complex problem-solving, and building Yahweh's worship altars.

Abigail Ebenezer-Gabriels, a Teacher, Business Leader, Strategy and Policy Expert, Executive Co-Founder at the Ebenezer Gabriels Teacher, Worshiper, and Multi-disciplinary leader in Business, Technology, Education, and Development. Blessed with prophetic teaching abilities with the anointing to unveil the mysteries in the Word of God. She is a Multi-specialty Keynote Speaker, with a special anointing to explain Heaven's ordinances on earth.

Ebenezer Gabriels & Abigail Ebenezer-Gabriels are married, and building worship altars for the Lord across industries.

About Ebenezer Gabriels

At Ebenezer Gabriels Ministries (EGM), we fulfill the mandate of building worship altars by sharing the story of the most expensive worship ever offered by Jesus Christ, the Son of God and dispersing the aroma of the knowledge of Jesus Christ to the ends of the world.

Ebenezer Gabriels Publishing delivers biblically grounded learning experiences that prepare audiences for launch into their prophetic calling. We create educational content and deliver in innovative ways through online classrooms, apps, audio, and prints to enhance the experience of each audience as they are filled with the aroma of Christ knowledge and thrive in their worship journey.

CONTACT

hello@ebenezergabriels.org
www.ebenezergabriels.org

Other Books by Ebenezer and Abigail Gabriels

Worship

Worship is Expensive

War of Altars

Business and Purpose

Unprofaned Purpose for Business

Elements of Time

Spirit of Teams

Kids

Activating my Prophetic Senses for Kids

Bree Learns about Processes

Places we went - Jerusalem

The Excellent Spirit of Daniel

The Birth of a King

Places we went - Uganda

Marriage

Heaven's Gate way to a Blissful marriage for Him

Heaven's Gateway to a Blissful marriage for Her

Deliverance from the Yokes of Marital Ignorance

Pulling Down the Strongholds of Evil Participants in Marriage

Prophetic

The Prophetic System

Activating Your Prophetic Senses

Dreams and Divine Interpretations

Relationships (singles)

Heaven's Compass for Cultivating a Blissful Pre-Marital Atmosphere for Her

Heaven's Compass for Cultivating a Blissful Pre-Marital Atmosphere for Him

Deliverance

Uncursed

Deliverance from the Yoke of Accursed Names

Deliverance from the Curse of Vashti

Deliverance from the Yoke of Incest

Deliverance from the Wrong Family Tree

Principles of Prophetic Deliverance

Mind

Deliverance from the Yokes Deep Mysteries of Creation in the Realms of Thoughts, Imaginations and Words

Spiritual War and Prayers

Blazing Sword of the Lord

Rapid Fire

The Big Process called Yoke

Deliverance of the Snares of the Fowler

The only Fire that Extinguishes Witchcraft

No longer Fugitives of the Earth

Subduers of the Earth

Prayers of the Decade

Manifold Mysteries of Water

Growth and Advancing in Faith

Men: Called out of the Dunghill

Women: Bearers of Faith

New Beginnings in Christ

Wisdom my Companion

Deeper Mysteries of the Blood

Nations and intercessions

The Scroll and the Seal

America: The Past, the Present and the Next Chapter

Herod: The Church and Nigeria

Prophetic Insights into the Year

21 Weapons of Survival for 2021

2022 Meet the God Who Saves Blesses Shepherds and Carries

Soul

Deeper Mysteries of the Soul (English, Spanish, Arabic and Chinese)

Unmute my Soul

Uncursed Series

The Spiritually Intelligent Mother

www.ingramcontent.com/pod-product-compliance
Lightning Source LLC
Chambersburg PA
CBHW022132080426
42734CB00006B/335